MONKEY WRENCH

New Quilts
from an Old Favorite

American Quilter's Society

P. O. Box 3290 • Paducah, KY 42002-3290
FAX 270-898-1173 *www.AQSquilt.com*

Located in Paducah, Kentucky, the American Quilter's Society (AQS) is dedicated to promoting the accomplishments of today's quilters. Through its publications and events, AQS strives to honor today's quiltmakers and their work and to inspire future creativity and innovation in quiltmaking.

EDITORS: BARBARA SMITH & SHELLEY HAWKINS
GRAPHIC DESIGN: LYNDA SMITH
COVER DESIGN: MICHAEL BUCKINGHAM
PHOTOGRAPHY: CHARLES R. LYNCH
             (UNLESS OTHERWISE NOTED)

Library of Congress Cataloging-in-Publication Data

Monkey wrench / by American Quilter's Society ; editor, Barbara Smith.
     p. cm. -- (New quilts from an old favorite)
   Includes bibiographical references and index.
     ISBN 1-57432-841-7
   1. Patchwork--Patterns. 2. Quilting. 3. Patchwork quilts--Competitions--United States.   I. Smith, Barbara, 1941- II. American Quilter's Society.   III. Series.

TT835.M648 2004
746.46'041--dc22

                                   2004001154

Additional copies of this book may be ordered from the American Quilter's Society, PO Box 3290, Paducah, KY 42002-3290; 800-626-5420 (orders only please); or online at www.AQSquilt.com. For all other inquiries, call 270-898-7903.

Sponsors

Thanks to the following sponsors:

Quality Polyester Products for Home and Industry

Because You Simply Love To Sew™

Dedication

This book is dedicated to all those who
view a traditional quilt block and see
within it a link to the past and a vision
for the future.

The Museum of the American Quilter's Society (MAQS)

An exciting place where the public can learn more
about quilts, quiltmaking, and quiltmakers.

Through collecting quilts and other programs,
MAQS focuses on celebrating and developing today's quiltmaking.

Whether presenting new or antique quilts, MAQS promotes
understanding of, and respect for, all quilts – new and antique,
traditional and innovative, machine made and handmade, utility and art.

Contents

Preface

While preservation of the past is a museum's primary function, its greatest service is performed as it links the past to the present and to the future. With that intention, the Museum of the American Quilter's Society (MAQS) sponsors an annual contest and exhibit called *New Quilts from an Old Favorite*.

Created to acknowledge our quiltmaking heritage and to recognize innovation, creativity, and excellence, the contest challenges today's quiltmakers to interpret a single traditional quilt block in a work of their own design. Each year contestants respond with a myriad of stunning interpretations.

Monkey Wrench: New Quilts from an Old Favorite is a wonderful representation of these interpretations. In this book you'll find a brief description of the 2004 contest, followed by a presentation of the five award winners and the 12 finalists and their quilts.

Full-color photographs of the quilts accompany each quiltmaker's comments – comments that provide insight into their widely diverse creative processes. Full-sized templates for the traditional Monkey Wrench block are included to form the basis for your own rendition. Tips, techniques, and patterns contributed by the contest winners offer an artistic framework for your own work.

Our wish is that *Monkey Wrench: New Quilts from an Old Favorite* will further our quiltmaking heritage as new quilts based on the Monkey Wrench block are inspired by the outstanding quilts, patterns, and instructions in this book.

The Contest

Although the contest encouraged unconventional creativity, there were some basic requirements for entries.

- Quilts entered in the contest were to be recognizable in some way as being related to the Monkey Wrench block.
- The finished size of the quilt was to be a minimum of 50" in width and height but could not exceed 100".
- Quilting was required on each quilt entered in the contest.
- A quilt could be entered only by the person(s) who made it.
- Each entry must have been completed after December 31, 1998.

To enter the contest, each quiltmaker was asked to submit an entry form and two slides of their quilt – one of the full quilt, and a second of a detail from the piece. In the *Monkey Wrench* contest, quiltmakers from around the world responded to the challenge.

Three jurors viewed dozens of slides, deliberating over design, use of materials, interpretation of the theme, and technical excellence. Eventually they narrowed the field of entries to 18 finalists who were invited to submit their quilts for judging.

With quilts by the 18 finalists assembled, three judges meticulously examined the pieces, eval-uating them again for design, innovation, theme, and workmanship. First- through fifth-place award winners were selected and notified.

Each year the *New Quilts from an Old Favorite* contest winners and finalists are featured in an exhibit that opens at the Museum of the American Quilter's Society in Paducah, Kentucky. Over a two-year period, the exhibit travels to a number of museums across North America and is viewed by thousands of quilt enthusiasts. Corporate sponsorship of the contest helps to underwrite costs, enabling even smaller museums across the country to display the exhibit.

Also, annually the contest winners and finalists are included in a beautiful book published by the American Quilter's Society. *Monkey Wrench: New Quilts from an Old Favorite* is the eleventh in the contest, exhibit, and publication series. It joins the following other traditional block designs used as contest themes: *Double Wedding Ring, Log Cabin, Kaleidoscope, Mariner's Compass, Ohio Star, Pineapple, Storm at Sea, Bear's Paw, Tumbling Blocks,* and *Feathered Star.*

For information about entering the current year's *New Quilts from an Old Favorite* contest, write to Museum of the American Quilter's Society at PO Box 1540, Paducah, KY, 42002-1540; call (270) 442-8856; or visit MAQS online at www.quiltmuseum.org.

Monkey Wrench Block

Each generation adds its own variations to quiltmaking. Names of quilt blocks, for instance, have had diverse translations throughout history. The Monkey Wrench design holds a fascinating twist in its interpretation.

This conventional block pattern became the symbol of freedom in our country's early quiltmaking. It is believed that traditional quilt patterns were given new meaning as African-American slaves used them to devise an elaborate code of escape. As part of the Underground Railroad, quilts featuring a succession of different blocks were hung outdoors during daylight to signal escape plans to other slaves. Marking the beginning of a life-changing journey, the Monkey Wrench pattern was the first to be displayed on the route to freedom. This quilt design was used to inform slaves to prepare the mental and spiritual tools they would need to carry on their escape.

The Monkey Wrench block is typically based on a Four-Patch, Equal Nine-Patch, Unequal Nine-Patch, or Square-in-a-Square block. Other common names for the block include Broken Plate, Churn Dash, Hole in the Barn Door, Shoo Fly, Snail's Trail, and Square and Compass. The variations in the design emerge from the block's numerous foundations. Two distinct versions, Snail's Trail and Churn Dash, are most frequently seen in this collection of quilts.

Upholding the integrity of the design, contestants skillfully varied the Monkey Wrench, giving it a unique and personal interpretation. Popular trends in this year's contest include the use of chenille, a red and black color palette, and elaborate hand quilting. Whether elongated, chenilled, latticed, or tiled, the Monkey Wrench block is a classic pattern that yields unlimited design possibilities.

Gwenfai Rees Griffiths

Abergele, North Wales, United Kingdom

MEET THE QUILTER

My favorite lesson in school was sewing. I made my own clothes before becoming hooked on patchwork, which happened after attending a quilt exhibition in 1992. Little did I realize how it would take over my life.

Over the years, I have made many different types of quilts, but now realize that I will never be able to make an art quilt. I am a traditionalist at heart, but have no wish to produce replicas and prefer to make my own contemporary quilts without losing the original impression. There is never a meaningful reason to any of my quilts. I make them because I want to. Quilting is a great outlet for creative expressions. My inspiration comes from various things, such as old quilts, fabric, or as in this case, a competition theme.

I enjoy every part of quiltmaking, from designing to the final stitch. I no longer need to have a clear picture of a quilt in my head before I start, especially when making a medallion quilt. The basic plan is there, but the shapes can be filled in as I go.

I was persuaded to teach a class at a local village several years ago. I thought after a couple of years, the students would have had enough, but they come every week, enjoying the patchwork and comradeship.

I have a bit of an obsession about curves in my quilts. I never start with the intention of having them, but they seem to appear.

Harlequin

71" x 71"

My family has always supported and encouraged me and doesn't complain, even when I go on my travels. I exhibit and compete internationally and have been fortunate to win awards in the United Kingdom, France, and United States. The challenge of competition is an excellent way to stretch my designing and sewing skills, and this is my second quilt to be juried into the museum contest.

I have made so many new friends through quilting and have traveled to other countries to find that quilters are the same friendly crowd. I often wonder what my life would be like if I hadn't gone to visit my first quilt exhibition in 1992.

INSPIRATION AND DESIGN

An Amish quilt has been on my must-make list for several years. When I discovered that the Monkey Wrench was a traditional Amish block, this competition was the ideal opportunity to combine the two.

For the layout of the quilt, I was drawn to a medallion because it offers so many options. The center can be planned and sewn before deciding on the outer elements of the quilt. The color choice was dictated by my limited stash of Primrose Gradation fabrics, which have a suede look. I wanted some dramatic colors to give the quilt visual impact.

I have a bit of an obsession about curves in my quilts. I never start with the intention of having them, but they seem to appear. Because the Monkey Wrench is a Nine-Patch, I decided to make nine blocks. Varying the size of the blocks changes the image dramatically. Because the center block would be double the size of the corner blocks, the other four blocks had to be rectangles.

CONSTRUCTING THE QUILT

I drew the layout to scale to check for balance. The Nine-Patch grids were accurately drafted on paper. I lightly sketched the lines of the Monkey Wrench block and, with a compass, drew the curves. The shapes were traced to template plastic. To keep these blocks accurate, I would have to hand piece, so a seam allowance was not added.

To square the medallion center, I decided that Flying Geese traveling outward was the best option. I drew the actual size of the corner and roughly drew in some lines to see how they looked. After several attempts, the final design was seven rows with the geese getting bigger as they went outward. I usually foundation piece on plain paper, but tried the freezer paper method this time. Cutting the fabric shapes with a seam allowance slightly larger than ¼" allowed for slight errors in placement. The freezer paper was easy to use because the pieces could be ironed in place after stitching and flipping the fabric.

After the corners were stitched to the center, I pinned the piece onto my design wall. What a pleasant surprise! It seemed to have a three-dimensional effect with the Flying Geese coming from behind the center panel.

Cutting curves

I decided to add curves to the inner border. To cut the curve, the following method was used instead of a paper pattern.

1. Cut the border fabric the length of the center panel by the desired width of the border plus the depth of the curve (e.g., 2").

2. Place the wrong side of the border fabric onto the right side of the center panel, extending it by 2".

3. With a sliver of soap, draw a fairly gentle curve. This can't be wider than the depth of the curve. Cut through both layers. Remove the excess strip of border fabric and place registration marks on both the center panel and the border.

4. Place the border and the center panel right sides together. Pin through the registration marks. Ease the curves into place and pin across the seam. This can be stitched by machine.

For the outer border, I could see that the lime green needed to be carried outward. Luckily, I had bought a pack of eight shades of lime green and didn't have enough of the ones used in the center, so I just chose another one. The outer borders were cut the same as the inner border.

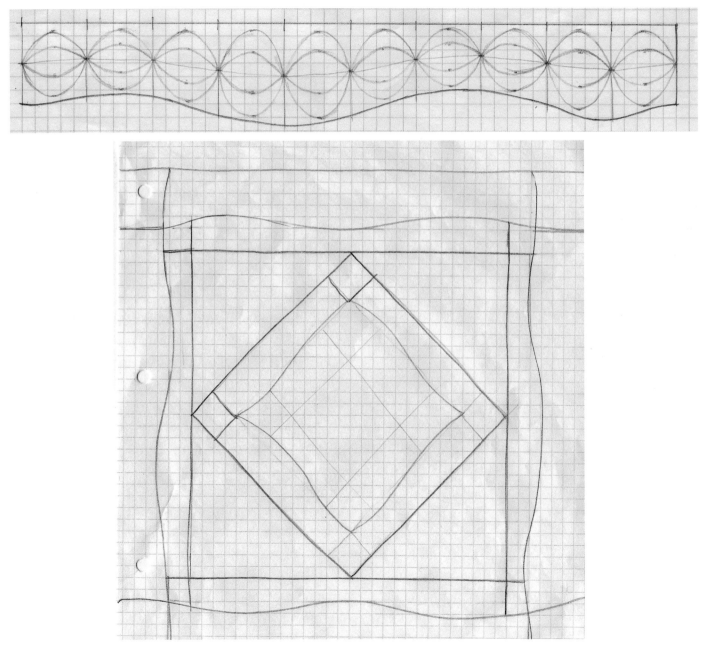

Gwenfai's original sketches for border and layout of HARLEQUIN

Quilting

Hand quilting is a an important part of the quilt to me and never an afterthought. I find it relaxing and quilt every evening without fail, even if it's only half an hour. At an exhibition, a quilt can draw you from a distance. I like the viewer to see another dimension that quilting adds when looking at it from close quarters.

The navy background of the three different-sized blocks formed interesting-shaped spaces, ideal for hand quilting. I knew feather patterns would be included because I couldn't possibly make an Amish quilt without them. The navy background shapes were traced onto paper, with feather shapes drawn into these. I found that my favorite quilting thread pulled the batting through to the surface of the quilt, so I changed brands.

The first and third borders were quilted with a scalloped pattern. To do this, I divided the length of the border into equal sizes with a sliver of soap as a marker. I drew a very wavy line along the center length. With the white pencil, a free-hand double scallop was drawn on the first border and a treble scallop on the third. The Flying Geese were quilted in the ditch. To fill the background shapes, I added a bit of Welsh quilting patterns.

It's recommended to repeat patterns in quilts if possible, so the final border had to be a feather pattern. I didn't relish the thought of making four separate feather template patterns and thought I'd have a go at drawing them directly on the border freehand, after a little practice of course. I drew one of the borders on paper and practiced drawing a feather pattern. After several attempts, I took the plunge and drew it directly onto the quilt.

The binding had to be cerise because this was the only fabric I had enough of. Before binding the quilt, I thought the edge looked a bit dull. To brighten it, I cut a strip of lime green, pressed it in half, and tacked it in place before binding. That looked much better, but it wasn't straight and, being a bright color, stood out like a sore thumb. I scalloped the edge every half inch by hand and was pleased with it. It looked as if it were planned from the beginning. Isn't it great how these things turn out?

Quilting Pattern in Navy Medallion Background

reverse pattern here

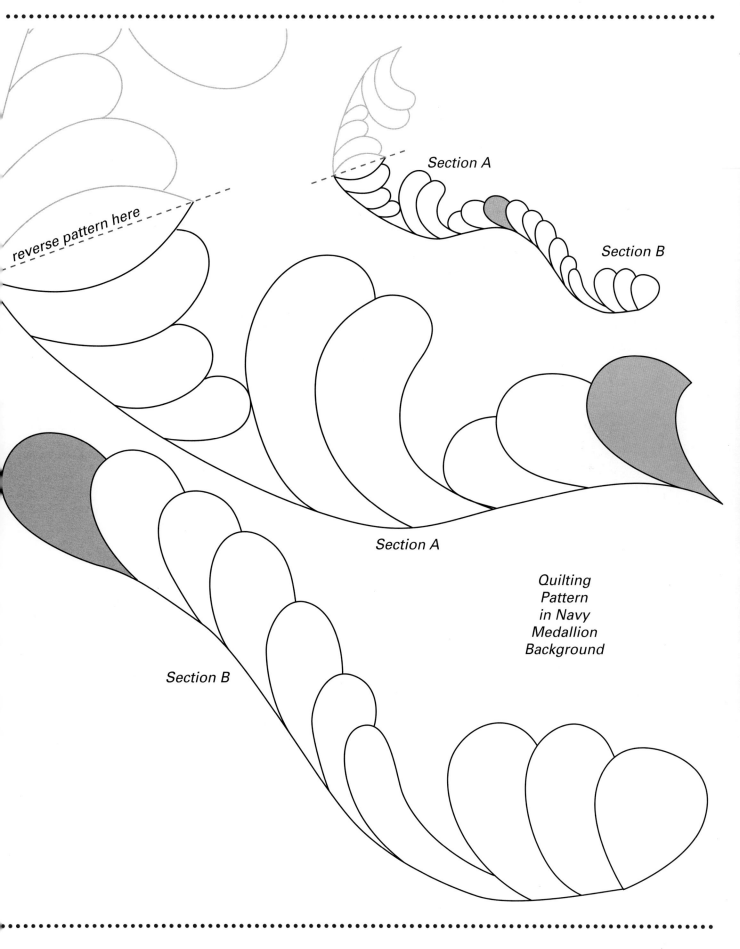

reverse pattern here

Section A

Section B

Section A

Section B

Quilting
Pattern
in Navy
Medallion
Background

2nd Place

Sherri Bain Driver

Centennial, Colorado

I am absolutely crazy about quilts and love every step of making them, from the initial idea to the final stitch in the binding — even the basting.

MEET THE QUILTER

Involved in some kind of sewing or needlework since the age of eight, I didn't get hooked on quilting until 1986. That year, my husband, two kids, and I moved back to Colorado after 11 years in the Navy. The kids were in elementary school, which provided a little time to myself to sew. I took a few classes at a local quilt shop and made some friends who introduced me to the wonderful world of quilt guilds, books, magazines, and shows.

I am absolutely crazy about quilts and love every step of making them, from the initial idea to the final stitch in the binding – even the basting. I read a lot of books and articles about quilts, attend quilt shows, and take classes on color, design, and assembly to gain a broad range of knowledge. Pictures that would make interesting quilts are clipped and filed. I like making quilts for contests. It's fun to work within a set of rules and I really need a deadline to push me to finish.

My sewing area is just a corner of our unfinished basement. It's not glamorous, but has everything I need, including a sewing machine, cutting area, open shelves for fabric, and a design wall. Many happy hours are spent there sewing, designing, or just looking at my fabric and dreaming about quilts I'd like to make. I've learned to make good use of even a few free minutes. Many of my quilts were made in small amounts of time here and there.

Monkey Business

55" x 55"

What began as a hobby for me has turned into a passion and profession. Through the years, I have taught quilting classes and have written patterns and two books. Now I am an editor for a quilting magazine. Even though my work is full-time, I make a few quilts each year and still teach occasionally.

INSPIRATION AND DESIGN

Designing and making innovative versions of traditional quilts is tremendously fun, so I eagerly anticipate the museum contest each year. There are a couple of different blocks called Monkey Wrench and I wondered which one the organizers were expecting. When I got the entry form with the Churn Dash and Snail's Trail blocks printed on it, I decided to play with a design incorporating both. I wasn't sure the two blocks would be compatible. One is drafted in a 4 x 4 grid and the other in a 5 x 5 grid, so their seam lines don't touch the block edges in the same place.

Designing on the computer is a quick way to try numerous ideas, but because much of my work day is spent at a computer, I'm not thrilled at the idea of sitting in front of one during my time off. A few initial sketches may be made on the computer, but incomplete designs are often printed so I can doodle in other parts by hand. I also don't want my quilt designs to be affected by my limited computer skills.

I've collected ikat fabrics for 15 years and have a huge stash. The designs on these fabrics are made by wrapping warp and/or weft threads to resist dyes before weaving. Done by hand, this process results in feathery edged motifs rather than the sharp exact color changes accomplished by printing. Some ikats are simple stripes or broken plaids with subtle color changes, and others have intricate multicolored motifs.

The last two quilts I made had earthy colors and such similar lines that some of my friends thought they were the same quilt. I needed to branch out! The first fabric chosen for MONKEY BUSINESS was the pink ikat in the largest triangles of the Churn Dash block. I searched through my stash for more ikats and stripes that would work with pink, then added a few hand-dyed fabrics.

Although the patches in the Churn Dash blocks can be rotary cut, templates were used to simplify centering fabric motifs and cutting identical repeats. The Snail's Trail blocks were foundation pieced.

I didn't have enough striped fabric for the entire border, so I searched fabric Web sites and was thrilled to find it. When the fabric arrived, it was a similar, but not identical stripe. I used it anyway. Did you notice that the left and top borders are a different stripe than the right and bottom borders?

DESIGNING THE QUILT

Designing on graph paper, I alternated the two different Monkey Wrench blocks. I imagined this would become a medallion-style design after drawing just a few of each block to make a small clump. With this sketch, I realized that I prefer the Churn Dash block turned on point to form an X. The diagonal setting also gave the Snail's Trail block more movement.

The edges of the blocks on point made me think of adding a zigzag border. I love zigzags and stripes, so they were sketched in too. With no idea how to assemble the drawn border, I hoped to figure it out by the time it would be assembled. While working on a design, I never worry about how to make the quilt because my design should not be limited by my sewing capabilities. I'm amazed how often a solution will pop up out of nowhere when needed.

I thought about this first design for several weeks and decided to see what would happen if the Snail's Trail block was stretched into a rectangle. Without the fuss of drawing several blocks on graph paper, I used the computer instead. Two of the block's arms were colored black, stretched, and duplicated across the page. I didn't want to make a quilt with so many Snail's Trail blocks or spend time at the computer refining shapes, colors, or values on my drawing. Instead, I placed tracing paper over the printout, traced the elongated blocks, and refined my design before cutting fabric.

I really liked the extra movement made by the elongated Snail's Trail blocks. On the printout, it was apparent that the spaces between the blocks could be filled with large and small Churn Dashes. The large white triangle of the Snail's Trail caught my interest. A striped fabric for that patch would accentuate the illusion of spinning. With a little math, I figured that 5" and 10" Churn Dash and Snail's Trail blocks, diagonally set, needed a fairly wide border to reach the required size for this contest. Great! I still had space for a zigzag border.

My design focused on the shape formed by four dark Snail's Trail arms surrounding a small Churn Dash. While tracing the shapes, I shaded just the parts with the strongest values, which are the darkest shapes that form the main quilt structure.

Sherri's original sketch of MONKEY BUSINESS

At the edges of the quilt design, the block coloring needed change to avoid partial designs, such as dark arms not attached to anything. I knew the value of the large Churn Dashes would mostly be medium and form a secondary pattern, so it wasn't necessary to color in my initial sketches.

The four center Snail's Trails were sewn first and pinned to the design wall. I cut patches for the Churn Dash blocks and added them a few at a time, evaluating color and value. With the triangles of the small Churn Dash matching the purple in the Snail's trail, the shapes merge to disguise the edges of the two blocks, adding more move-ment to the design. I cut patches to audition for the remaining blocks to reach a pleasing design, then assembled them.

ELONGATED BLOCK ASSEMBLY

To make a template for the center diamonds, photocopy or trace the foundation pattern. On transparent template plastic, trace one of the center diamonds, adding a ¼" seam allowance. Cut the diamond out. With this template, cut and piece four diamonds. Press the seam allowances open. Center this unit on the wrong side of the foundation in the space for Unit 1 and pin in place. Foundation piece the rest of the block.

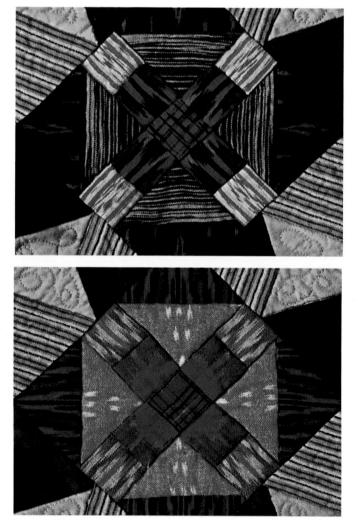

Detail of small Churn Dash blocks

Detail of elongated block

**Full-sized elongated
MONKEY BUSINESS block**

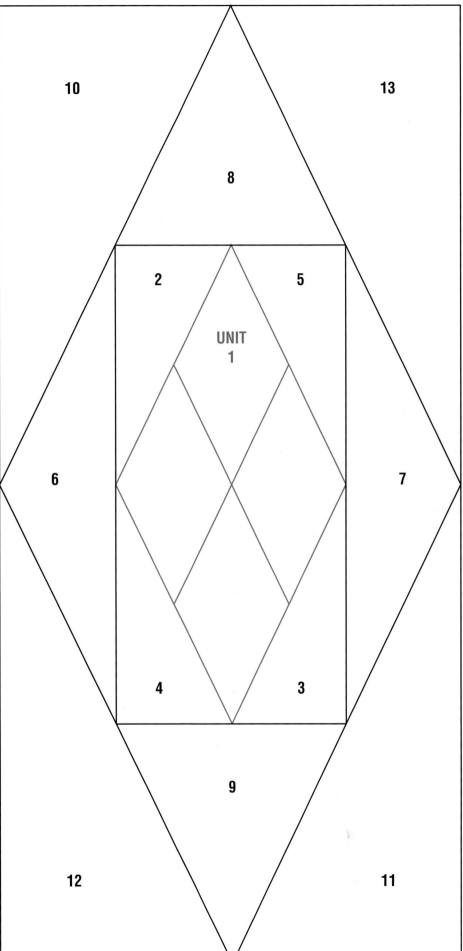

To keep grain lines in the right place and save fabric, I make templates for the foundation patches, adding ½" seam allowances all around. When the block is finished, trim ¼" from the printed outer line.

Patricia Dowling

Callahan, Florida

MEET THE QUILTER

While spending time with my grandparents as a child, they had stacks of quilts around the house for me to play and sleep on. I learned needlework from my grandmother and was happy that she took the time to teach me about saving material. I created usable items while learning to apply what she taught. Saving material continues for me today, but I always find more when shopping.

While in the United States Air Force, I met and married a young man who was in the Air Force as well. I decided to be a stay-at-home wife and mother. We raised two daughters and traveled around the country and world. After 20 years in the military, we retired to Florida and now have four grandchildren and two great-grandchildren.

I have made quilts for the family and even the family pets. My husband usually asks if I'm sure I need more fabric because the walls are insulated with quilts throughout the house. He calls the wallhangings "wall warmers." My bed has a different quilt for every month of the year.

All the quilts I've made for my family are well used. My grandson took one camping, claiming he could not sleep without it. I just make the children new quilts when they become worn. My grandchildren tell me that my house smells like quilts. Obviously, I sew more than cook.

Sometimes, I dream of the subject matter to design. Other times, the fabric tells me what to do. I choose simple designs because of my down-to-earth nature.

Safe Harbor

56" x 72"

I am lucky to have thoughtful family and friends. When my daughter asked what I wanted for my birthday, pink fabric was my answer. She gave me a box with six different shades of pink, six yards each. My sister-in-law gave me a fat quarter of fabric for every year of my age. As for birthdays, the more the merrier.

I attend monthly meetings at quilt guilds in Jacksonville, Florida. It's almost 100 miles round trip. I live on a winding, sandy road and sometimes have to take our four-wheel drive to get out and back again. A few of my friends came to visit and decided the reason I get so much sewing done is because of my isolated area. I'm lucky to have quilting friends for phone visits and to exchange patterns and ideas through the mail.

The type of quilt I love the best is traditional and the ones I most enjoy creating are the challenge quilts. The design relays my feelings through color and fabric. Sometimes, I dream of the subject matter to design. Other times, the fabric tells me what to do. I choose simple designs because of my down-to-earth nature.

I enjoy living in the country with quiet time to design and construct quilts. My piecing and quilting is done on home sewing machines and I have useful quilting tools organized and ready to use. Almost every day is a quilting day. Even on vacation, I find some quilting activity to enjoy. Family members all know to visit me when they have something that requires sewing.

INSPIRATION AND DESIGN

When I first drew the Monkey Wrench block and turned it on point, it resembled water. At this point, I had no idea of direction and considered the project for a couple of days. A boat harbor came to mind because the water looked so rough.

I decided on the size and drew the blocks to see how many would be required. With some idea of how much to purchase, I began looking for fabric. After a few trips to many stores, I purchased material and drew from my own stash as well. A few blocks were completed and placed on the design wall. I decided to move a half square down on each row and liked the design better. With this idea, I drew the entire quilt to scale with simple ships in the harbor, and I could see the quilt taking shape. The Churn Dash pattern was used for the stars to guide ships to harbor.

The fabric I had purchased for the city background did not complement the blue in the water and sky. Luckily, there was some yellow in my stash left from my granddaughter's quilt. It worked and inspired me to name the quilt SAFE HARBOR. The blue moon was also a scrap. Seven flags were added to the masts of the sailing ships for luck. The color of the ships just seemed to work. The fabric chosen was not large enough and after searching a number of shops, not one had the fabric, so I had to slightly change the design.

My patterns are drafted with a mechanical pencil and I take care to measure correctly. Rotary cutters are wonderful tools as long as you take your time and make an exact cut. As the old saying goes, measure twice and cut once. This is a good philosophy for saving fabric and producing satisfactory results. I draw the pattern to finished size, add ¼" seam allowances, and estimate fabric yardage with the use of a calculator.

I have three computer programs for laying out colors and making changes. However, my patterns are drafted by hand because I prefer simple lines. Every quilt has a story and when the story is told, the quilt is finished. Even the quilting plays a part in the theme of the quilt.

I machine quilted many different designs throughout the quilt. Having several fishing and boating collectibles, my daughter liked the design and wants me to make a smaller version of the quilt for her family room. I look forward to designing her quilt with the knowledge gained from SAFE HARBOR.

No matter how long I have been quilting, something new is learned on each and every project. I was challenged and rewarded as a participant in this contest.

Patricia's original sketch of SAFE HARBOR

Sue Turnquist

Kalamazoo, Michigan

MEET THE QUILTER

In March of 2003, I moved into my dream studio, having no idea what the year had in store for me. Little did I know this quilt would my last made-in-Missouri project. I have been quilting approximately eight years, all of which have been in my Missouri home.

My husband and I were both associate professors in veterinary pathology. After 18 years in higher education, job circumstances nudged us into looking at other employment opportunities. We spent much of the summer on the road, interviewing with various universities and private industry. We decided to pull up roots and give private industry a try. In our profession, this is very much akin to starting from scratch. Talk about a midlife crisis!

In a period of less than two months, my husband and I found a house in Michigan, sold ours in Missouri, packed and moved two households including my mother's, and started new jobs. We arrived on Saturday and began work on Monday. To say my life has been stressful is an understatement.

Leaving my quilting friends in Missouri has been particularly hard. I've had mini-retreats with the same group of women from my guild for years. This wonderful group of ladies will never know how much they've meant to me. Prior to my departure, we got together to

My quilts tend to have a life of their own and often evolve in their own way, so I seldom if ever have a quilt that turns out exactly like the original design.

Pinwheels & Whirligigs

56" x 56"

share dinner as well as photos from our first retreat. They surprised me with a gift certificate from a quilt shop in Michigan. We cried, hugged, and made plans to meet in Paducah. Quilters are truly phenomenal people.

I visited the local quilt shops during my job interview. I really do have to have my priorities straight. I haven't had the opportunity to visit the local guild, but eagerly anticipate the first meeting. I know they will make me as much at home in Michigan as I was with the Booneslick Trail Quilt Guild in Missouri.

INSPIRATION AND DESIGN

I have always loved the Snail's Trail pattern, but this was the first time I had worked with the block. Starting from scratch, quilt design software was used to create the basic block in grayscale (fig. 1). With no preconceived notions, I proceeded to a monochrome color scheme and auditioned other simple blocks in tandem with the Snail's Trail (fig. 2).

By starting with a simple pinwheel in the center and adding blocks to the periphery, the illusion of pinwheels and whirligigs was created. Numerous different blocks were tried as connectors for the larger whirligig blocks. I settled on the diagonal strip block that offered the illusion of framing, sashing, or crosshatching within the center medallion (fig. 3, page 27).

My goal was to incorporate blocks that could be easily paper pieced so I could use foundation pattern software to help in the screening process. This software was used to print the selected blocks on paper foundations as well.

Fabric selection was ongoing, but began in earnest once the design was more or less final-

Fig. 1. Computer design of basic block

Fig. 2. Monochrome color scheme

ized. My quilts tend to have a life of their own and often evolve in their own way, so I seldom if ever have a quilt that turns out exactly like the original design. I selected olive-colored fabrics for the background because of the wide selection of values in my stash. I knew a good selection of medium and light background fabrics would be needed. I continued to play with the color scheme on the computer, but much of the color selection was made during the construction process (fig. 4).

When designing a project that requires free-form piecing, such as the setting corners in this quilt, I start with a large piece of white paper cut to the exact finished size. The desired design is drawn for one piece, then I use a light table to trace the remaining pieces. Registration marks are added to the paper templates to facilitate reassembly.

Stripes that were crossed and strip-pieced were used for the inner and outer borders. The Snail's Trail blocks in the middle border and the wood and basket weave boxes were all paper-pieced. The papers for each corner were cut apart and used as templates and a spray adhesive was used to apply them to the back of the fabric. The free-form pieces were assembled with the aid of a light box and joined with invisible thread and a tiny zigzag topstitch.

Ruche flowers were added to the center of each whirligig to enhance illusion. They were constructed with tubes of gold batik, which were marked at half-inch intervals, then basted from one mark to the next while alternating sides. The thread was pulled to a crinoline foundation. After the excess foundation was trimmed, the finished flower was applied to the whirligig with a central bead and heavy-duty bead thread.

Fig. 3. Diagonal block with sashing illusion

Fig. 4. Determining color scheme

5th Place

Ann Horton

Redwood Valley, California

MEET THE QUILTER

I am an Illinois farm girl, transplanted to the mountains of rural northern California. This is significant in my creative life because I have always been surrounded by country life. The greatness of God's creation and an attitude of where there's a will, there's a way is reflected in my quilt art.

My grandmother was a quilter. She made hundreds of quilts for Lutheran World Relief, plus a couple for me. I remember threading needles and playing under her quilt frame as a young girl. At age six, I began sewing and have sewn about everything from doll dresses to three-piece suits.

Along with sewing, I was the artist in the family. My art consisted of painting, collages, drawing, handwork, and stained glass. I dabbled in quilting, but waited until I became a wife and mother to get serious. When my daughter was born, I made and hand quilted a full-sized Birds in Air bed quilt. I set up the quilt frame in her bedroom and quilted while she took naps. This quilt was my entrée into the passion of quilting. I am serious about my quilting and devote some 20 hours a week to my art. My studio/sewing room is a special place of creativity and ideas for me.

Being a quilter speaks of commitment, passion, acknowledgment of beauty and creativity, and an awareness of the world as an abundant opportunity for choice.

Summer's Salute to Amelia

56" x 69"

In my professional life, I am a psychotherapist. Quilts adorn my office walls and I have watched while patients relate to the love, commitment, and time they know went into the work. I think they feel that if my art reflects this devotion, I will "go the journey" with them as well. Being a quilter speaks of commitment, passion, acknowledgment of beauty and creativity, and an awareness of the world as an abundant opportunity for choice.

I have made many quilts, both traditional and contemporary. Each one contains a hundred or more different fabrics. The essence of fabric and color is thrilling and the array of choices is dazzling and seductive. Beading, embellishment, threads, and of course the quilting itself all add to the banquet of senses that a quilt represents.

Quilts have a language of their own. They speak of emotion, meditation, laughter, and sometimes tears both in the making and the finished product. I get intensely caught up in the creative process. Thinking and dreaming in quilts, I often awake in the middle of the night with a piece of the puzzle falling into place. This process can be attributed to my faith. I believe that creativity is God's gift, that He delights in our happy use of this gift, and often gets involved with us in the creation.

One of the amazing aspects of quilting is the connection it brings to others. We are blessed to have opportunities to share our work with a national and international community. The relationship between the quilter and the industry is astonishing. On a more intimate level, I rejoice at the closeness of friendships and creative sharing that come from my 12-member quilt group, Mendocino Quilt Artists. The laughter, tears, and honest encouragement from these women have a significant impact in my life.

My hope is to grow and explore through quilting for as long as I am able to lift needle to fabric. With heartfelt gratitude, I appreciate all the pieces that make this possible.

INSPIRATION AND DESIGN

This quilt resulted from a challenge between friends. My long-time friend and quilt pal, Laura Fogg, traveled with me to the American Quilter's Society Quilt Exposition in Nashville in 2003. Looking at the *New Quilts from an Old Favorite* exhibit there, we agreed to both make a quilt for the Monkey Wrench contest.

It was Labor Day weekend, I was planning to travel out of the country until mid-September, and the quilt needed to be ready for photography by mid-October. Never one to turn down an impossible challenge, I envisioned design possibilities on the plane ride home from Nashville.

The image of a small, vintage-looking reproduction quilt came to mind. I had made this quilt a couple years earlier in the Monkey Wrench pattern to honor my great-great grandmother, Amelia Kahle. Amelia emigrated from Germany to the American heartland to homestead a farm in 1870. I grew up on that same farm. Making the small quilt to honor her roots and contribution in my life had been a pleasure. Why couldn't I use that old quilt in a new quilt set with my own homestead?

The kinship I felt with Amelia's efforts to carve out a home in a new land had been cemented when my husband and I built a new home on our mountain property in California. The split rail fence in our orchard became the setting for Amelia's quilt. Our mountains would be in the background, and the sky and earth would sing a salute to Amelia by softly reflecting the quilt pattern.

I gathered dozens of pale-morning-light fabrics and pieced many blocks, blending the colors to look like a soft breeze and swirl of clouds. I appliquéd purple and blue mountain ridges before assembling the meadow. The split rail fence was such fun! Because I would appliqué Amelia's quilt onto the new one, more dimensional appliqué around the quilt would help "settle" it into the setting.

The fence posts and rails were made by applying layers of raw-edged fabric over batting and thick felt, then quilting them together. I was able to "saw and nail" the fence into place in the same manner I had helped my husband build our own fence. Background hollyhocks seemed a natural choice. They had always been part of my Illinois farm, and we had continued to grow these sentinels in our mountain garden. These, too, were formed separately and appliquéd to the quilt. Hand beading was added later.

The quilt just grew from there. Inner piped border, more pieced blocks in the foreground, a tangle of weeds and embroidered flowers, and pieces of fallen oak branches among the wildflowers were added. The squirrel was pure playfulness and utilized a new technique of thread painting I developed this year. I like my pictorial quilts to tell a story, and the squirrel does this as he holds a freshly plucked plum from the orchard.

The summer sky and earth seem to celebrate Amelia's quilt, and I am pleased with the work

accomplished to weave Amelia's legacy into my own. A final note: the quilt was photographed on October 12, and I made the deadline!

THREAD PAINTING

Earlier this year, I made a quilt with a thread-painted Steller's Jay for the American Quilter's Society Lewis and Clark contest. Fascinated by the intricate shading and realistic features produced, I explored the technique of manipulating fabric under the machine's needle.

In my quilt of wild animals in our mountain garden, I gained experience while thread painting deer, raccoons, and other critters. It helped me learn through trial and error the approach I used to make the squirrel in this quilt. Most viewers want to touch the

Ann draws her inspiration for thread painting from nature photos.

squirrel because he looks so lifelike. The layers and patterns of the thread and stitches effectively form shaded fur and features that look authentic.

Quilt detail of hollyhocks. See inspiration photo on page 31.

Quilt detail of the squirrel

For this technique, be prepared to use a lot of thread and practice a lot of patience. Finding a photo of the animal or object is helpful in making the preliminary sketch. When drawing the animal, imagine it placed in the quilt to envision a pose that fits the setting. Make an outline sketch in the desired size of the finished animal, keeping in mind that thread painting shrinks the design somewhat.

The base of the design is made up of backing fabric, which will not show on the quilt, and a flat and sturdy batting. Trace the pattern on the batting with a pencil, adding simple details such as eyes, legs, etc. Gather fabrics that suggest the appropriate colors of the animal. Cut out sections of the animal and place them over the line drawing on the batting, overlapping fabrics. Pin a piece of netting over the entire animal to hold the

Ann's original outline sketch of a squirrel

loose fabric in place. This helps glide the needle and thread over the animal, making it easier to manipulate the piece for detail.

Set your machine for free-motion quilting with nylon thread in the bobbin and rayon thread on top. Begin sewing with a base color over the various areas. The actual thread painting involves layering different-colored threads in the direction the fur lies. The gray fur of the squirrel may have shades of black, white, and brown to make it more realistic. Highlighting special features like the eyes, nose, mouth, whiskers, and feet makes the animal come to life.

It is helpful to vary the stitch length and direction to make the tail fur longer and more prominent, for instance, and the face fur shorter and refined.

When thread painting is complete, the entire animal has been layered repeatedly with thread. Carefully cut out the animal close to the stitching edge, place it on the quilt, and free-motion "paint" it into place with more strokes of fur.

This technique is useful not only for animals and birds, but for tree limbs, cones, and other details. Learning to control the machine to make it a painting tool takes confidence and imagination. As with any technique, the more experienced I become, the more I refine and expand the steps.

One of the most delightful aspects of quilting is the never-ending parade of ideas and skills to explore. I've always been a hands-on learner, and what better media to satisfy the senses than fabric and thread.

Photograph of Ann's orchard that inspired SUMMER'S SALUTE TO AMELIA

Maggie Ball

Bainbridge Island, Washington

MEET THE QUILTER

I was born and raised in the north of England near the Scottish border, and moved to the United States with my husband, Nigel, in 1983. When we lived in Fayetteville, Arkansas, I discovered quilts and was thrilled to see them displayed on clotheslines outside farmhouses on the back roads in the Ozarks.

I began quilting in 1986 under the guidance of members of QUILT, the Northwest Arkansas quilt group. The endless design possibilities, as well as the joys of sharing a common interest with other enthusiasts, made quilting most appealing. At the Arkansas Quilters' Guild, I met several exceptionally talented quilters whose innovative approaches to both traditional and contemporary quilting were inspiring and influential.

We now live in the Pacific Northwest, an area rich in quilters and quilt stores. At my son's elementary school, I helped make quilts with all 20 classes as a fund-raiser. The projects were designed to complement the curriculum. Age and skill-level appropriate techniques, ranging from drawing and painting on fabric to hand sewing, were selected. The enthusiasm and creativity of the kids was delightful.

Maggie's photo by Mark Frey

While I had heard various eminent quilters discussing the merits of working in a series, it was something I had never tried ... Now I can speak from experience and highly recommend this adventure.

Caution, Zebra Crossing!

53½" x 53½"

For the last couple of years, I have been teaching quilting basics to middle school children through a series of machine projects, ranging from simple patchwork pillows and baby blankets, to larger, more complex lap quilts. The energy and uninhibited approach of children is exciting and refreshing. My work with children has led to the publication of my two books, *Creative Quilting with Kids*, and *Patchwork and Quilting with Kids* (Krause Publications, 2001 and 2003).

My next major project is planning a trip to Mongolia, where I have been invited to teach quilting in the capital city of Ulaanbaatar. Since the fall of communism, there has been severe economic stress, especially for urban Mongolians. The Japanese chapter of UNIFEM, an international organization assisting women worldwide, is establishing a center in Ulaanbaatar. It will provide a place for needy women to meet, have childcare facilities, and attend classes. The goal is to boost morale and offer new productive activities, which may in turn provide economic benefits.

I am a consultant with David Textiles Inc. to help design lines of fabric that appeal to young, and young-at-heart, quilters. I'm fortunate to receive encouragement and support for my work from many people in the quilting industry who are enthusiastic about teaching the next generation.

I love to teach quilting to all ages, enjoy making art quilts, have had my quilts exhibited both nationally and internationally, and am a certified quilt show judge with the Northern California Quilt Council. When I'm not quilting, I tend my garden and sing in a couple of choirs. My husband and I enjoy birdwatching and being outdoors in our beautiful Pacific Northwest surroundings.

INSPIRATION AND DESIGN

My quilt title has a double meaning. It was going to be simply ZEBRA CROSSING!, but I discovered that most Americans are not familiar with zebra crossings. A friend suggested adding CAUTION to provide a hint. In England, pedestrian crossings used to be called zebra crossings. Each end was marked by a black and white striped pole with an orange light perched atop. These beacons have now been replaced by traffic lights heralding the pedestrian crossing, but for many of us, the term zebra crossing lingers.

My inspiration germinated from "The Meetin' Place" article in the July/August 2003 issue of *Quilter's Newsletter Magazine.* In the article, Margaret Rolfe introduced Judy Hooworth of Sydney, Australia, along with five of her beautiful quilts. There were two lattice quilts, and the concept of dividing simple quilt blocks with lattice excited me. I could use all sorts of weird looking fabric combinations, and separate them with the narrow lattice strips. Also, there were numerous possibilities for creating patterns with lattices extending across the block boundaries.

While I had heard various eminent quilters discussing the merits of working in a series, it was something I had never tried. This quilt is the fourth in my series of lattice quilts. I didn't deliberately embark on the series, but became intrigued by the method and felt the desire to continue exploring the possibilities. Now I can speak from experience and highly recommend this adventure.

The first quilt was a simple Nine-Patch lattice and each quilt that followed became more intricate and challenging. I progressed to a Shoofly variation lattice and experimented with a brightly colored lattice in a pattern superimposed over all nine blocks. The third quilt was an Ohio Star, in which hand-dyed fabrics covered a wide spectrum of colors. This time, the wide sashing strips were split between the blocks to make a double sashing. Miniature blocks were used for the outer cornerstones of the quilt and prairie points were added to pep up the border.

STAR STRUCK, 53" x 53", designed and pieced by Maggie Ball, the third in her series of lattice quilts. Quilted by Wanda Rains, Kingston, Washington. Photo by Mark Frey.

The next step was to become even bolder with my use of color for the Monkey Wrench block. The combination of black, white, and red is always stunning. I had just completed a black-and-white Log Cabin variation with a dash of primary colors and felt ready for the challenge. The dotted and striped black-and-white fabrics begged to participate, so I decided to combine them with red and yellow to see what emerged. The dots and stripes

played off one another to enhance the design and there were plenty of options for their orientation.

I have great difficulty in preventing myself from arranging everything symmetrically, hence the nine blocks are strictly organized and balanced. However, when the sashing was added, I included red rectangles adjacent to the sashing intersections to create more Monkey Wrenches that crossed the boundaries of the blocks. This made the quilt asymmetrical and I debated long and hard about changing it to restore the symmetry. These new Monkey Wrenches really got into the works. There were too many red triangles in odd places, but at the same time, they added a certain tension to the design, which persuaded me that they should stay.

The zebras poked their noses in, but it was not until the borders were added that the quilt name came to me. By coincidence, I was reading *Life of Pi*, by Yann Martel. In this bizarre story, 16-year-old Pi finds himself at sea in a lifeboat with a spotted hyena, a wounded zebra, an orangutan, and a 450-pound Bengal tiger. If you haven't read the book, I'll leave the outcome to your imagination. Was it chance, or a subconscious decision to pit the spots against the stripes in this Monkey Wrench setting? Who knows!

CONSTRUCTING THE QUILT

Nine-Patch lattice quilts are easy and quick to piece. The challenge is in the fabric choice and value placement. I encourage you to lighten up and experiment with a variety of options. It really is fun.

To start a simple Nine-Patch lattice, cut nine squares each of nine fabrics. Arrange the squares so that each fabric appears in three of the nine blocks: the four corners, the four sides, and the center square.

Careful selection of pale lattices and dark sashing strips can produce stunning results with an illusion of three-dimensional layers. Lattice patterns can cross the boundaries of the blocks and give coherence to the overall design. I like to use solid, tonal, or small-print monochromatic fabrics in the lattice to separate the square units within the block. Using one fabric for all of the intersecting squares of the lattice provides continuity between the blocks.

My lattice quilts follow the same basic pattern of nine Nine-Patch blocks fragmented by narrow lattice strips and separated by sashing. The original 10½" blocks become 12" blocks when the ¾" lattice strips are inserted. Each of the nine square units has a finished size of 3½". Any Nine-Patch block can be drafted to these dimensions. The cutting sizes for one Monkey Wrench block with a lattice are provided below.

The 2" wide split sashing is strip pieced from two 1½" strips and has red rectangles next to the four sashing cornerstones in the center of the quilt top.

By extending the split sashing into the border, the long side border pieces, except the outer black ones, are less than 42" and can be cut across a full width of fabric. This avoids the necessity of piecing border strips, or the frustration of not having enough fabric to cut them lengthwise. The narrow black and white border is actually a folded strip inserted into the seam between the yellow and the red. The quilting stitches tether the strip in alternate directions to produce a wavy effect.

Piece	Quantity	Cutting
A	1	4" square
B	12	1¼" x 4"
C	4	1¼" square
D	8	2¼" x 4"
E	4	4⅜" square, cut once diagonally

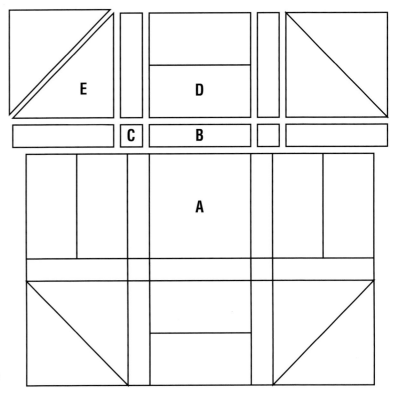

Block Assembly

After attaching the yellow and red borders to the quilt, I felt that there was too much red. The prairie points break up the red and bring the themes of triangles and stripes into the perimeter. I used a variety of sizes to add interest. When striped squares are folded to make prairie points, there are vertical stripes on one side of the triangle and horizontal stripes on the other, so you can choose which is the most appropriate.

The quilting pattern in the center field of the quilt is a large Monkey Wrench sewn in black and silver twisted thread, superimposed over all the blocks. First I stabilized the block grid with quilting in the ditch and serpentine stitching in the split sashing. The outer edge of the Monkey Wrench is defined with a double stitching line and parallel lines follow the rectangles and triangles of the pattern. The center block has a cross-hatch that is echoed in the outer triangles and rectangles. I used silver thread in the red border, adding more triangles to continue the peaks created by the prairie points and perpetuate the triangle theme.

The back of the quilt is pieced with a large Monkey Wrench block. I tend to buy fabric in one yard or half-yard chunks, so I rarely have enough of one fabric for an entire quilt back. I use large patches to minimize the number of seams because this makes quilting easier and reduces the chance of puckering. The Monkey Wrench block is 36" square and the side panels provide the extra breadth and width needed to complete the back.

Web site: dragonflyquilts.com
E-mail: maggieball@bainbridge.net

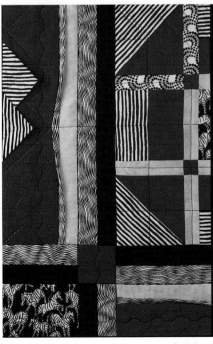

Split sashing and wavy folded border strip.
Photo by Mark Frey.

Back of CAUTION, ZEBRA CROSSING! Photo by Mark Frey.

Christine N. Brown & J. Renée Howell

Castle Rock, Colorado   Centennial, Colorado

An old adage proclaims that diamonds are a girl's best friend. In WHEEL OF FORTUNE, the Monkey Wrench befriends the diamond to explore a new facet of a traditional pattern.

MEET THE QUILTERS

Christine N. Brown: Since that fateful day when I purchased my first quilting magazine, every aspect of my life has been enriched, expanded, and challenged. I have worn the hat of student, teacher, designer, writer, editor, photographer, guild president, quilt museum board member, event planner, fund raiser, exhibit curator, committee chairperson, boutique buyer, consignor, statistician, quilt judge, and prolific purchaser of fabric.

Sometimes, I think about how many more quilts I could have produced if not for my volunteer involvement these last 30 years, but hope that my efforts have made a contribution to preserving and celebrating our quilting heritage. My personal reward has been the friendships and associations garnered through those years of activities.

Like other quiltmakers, I gravitated to quilting after many years of sewing garments and never looked back. In 1985, a national quilt magazine published one of my original designs. That encouraged me to write about quilts and develop patterns, and I am a still a frequent contributor to quilting magazines and other publications. My studio has natural lighting and features scenic vistas of the Colorado Rocky Mountains.

In 1997, I was designated a National Quilting Association Certified Quilt Judge. This has given me

Wheel of Fortune

61" x 61"

huge appreciation for quilts in which each of the design elements enhance the others to produce a beautifully integrated and unified piece of textile art. Through judging, I have been privileged to be up close and personal with some of the best work being done in quilting today.

The title, WHEEL OF FORTUNE, alludes to the uncertainty and unpredictability that march with us through life. As the wheel of my life has spun and stopped in unexpected and sometimes unwanted places, there have always been family and friends to offer love, comfort, and stability. None of us can choose how life will treat us or where that wheel of fortune will stop, but we can choose who we turn to in times of difficulty and how we respond to new directions and challenges.

J. Renée Howell: Lines of sewn thread have fascinated me from the moment I began to sew. As the rhythm of the needle, thread, and bobbin created the long seams required for a pair of slacks, I would be dreaming of something to sew that needed a lot of thread lines. I eventually abandoned seamstress work for the creative world of quilting. Purchasing a longarm machine answered my early yearnings.

Quilting Chris' original designs provides me with an outlet for my creative thread line urge. As Chris nears the final stages of sewing her quilt, she e-mails me a digital photograph. Placing tracing paper over the picture, I begin lightly sketching quilting designs with a mechanical pencil. My goal is to enhance her wonderful sense of color and design. With each quilt top, I design a new free-form pattern. A warm-up period of sketches continues until the right idea settles into my thoughts, then flows onto the tracing paper, which is more of a gift than a skill.

Once Chris delivers the quilt top, I pin it on my design wall to audition thread colors, much like quilters audition fabric for a top. I arrange the thread on the quilt to mimic possible quilting designs. The quilt top usually spends a week or so on my design wall as I sort through the possibilities. Due to the nature of longarm machines, I have learned to contemplate design ideas. Five minutes of sewing can result in two hours of removing stitches. My mantra is "Just because you can do something, doesn't mean you should. Think about it."

INSPIRATION AND DESIGN

Christine N. Brown: An old adage proclaims that diamonds are a girl's best friend. In WHEEL OF FORTUNE, the Monkey Wrench befriends the diamond to explore a new facet of a traditional pattern.

Creating visual movement and an interesting composition is always my goal in design. I chose the Snail's Trail version of Monkey Wrench and set about drafting this block into an elongated and elegant 60-degree diamond. I thought this would offer more options and help translate a square block into the circular vision I had in mind.

The center part of my design came together quickly and afforded many color and value options. Continuing from there was harder than I ever imagined. I chose fabrics, cut and sewed, then looked at the completed center from my design wall for over four months. No amount of thought, inspiration, or determination could help that quilt grow and finish itself.

Finally, I began to think outside the box, or in this case, outside the center square, and realized I had created a visual circle that could only be framed with another circle. I drafted a quarter-circle the actual size needed on paper, then made templates.

My preferred method of construction when accuracy is critical involves cutting templates to the finished size of each pattern piece. After completing the outer pieced ring, I trimmed the square center medallion into a circle shape, adding seam allowances, and pieced the two circles together. By changing the background fabric from light to medium green in the outer ring, the center image became the focal point.

Repeating shapes from the center image, I wanted a floating effect for the corners and added the dark green bars, again changing the background fabric from medium to dark green. After evaluating the completed top for another few weeks, I added appliquéd circles to punctuate and enliven the circular design.

CREATING THE CENTER MEDALLION

Christine N. Brown: Drafting the Monkey Wrench within a 60-degree diamond adds narrow angles and puts a different spin, both literally and figuratively, on the the blocks when joined. Set-in seams must be used to join the diamonds and all measurements have to be exact to eliminate distortion in the finished top.

The technique of using templates to mark fabric pieces with the sewing line takes more time initially, but allows accurate piecing of difficult or irregular blocks. It is basically a hand-piecing technique done by machine. Templates help with block stability by enabling the straight grain of fabric to be used on the outer and long edges.

Six blocks of one color combination were made for the inner medallion, then six in another combination for the outer medallion. The blocks were pieced with set-in seams. To accomplish this, I placed the blocks right sides together and inserted a pin straight through the corner, exactly aligning both top and bottom pieces. Additional pins were used to secure the stitching line and the "aligning" pin was removed. Each seam was sewn on the marked line from point to point, with one or two backstitches at each end. This is when it is handy to have the sewing lines marked; precision is important. Do not sew into the seam allowances when joining set-in seams.

To turn the completed hexagon into a square, corners were added. I measured the exact finished length of one side of the hexagon without including seam allowances. I drew a line exactly this length on my fabric, then marked a 30-degree angle on one end and a 60-degree angle on the other. These lines were extended until they met in a 90-degree corner. Two corner units were drawn in this fashion, then reversed for the other side. It is important that the right-angled corner stay on the straight grain of fabric. The long sides of the corner triangles were sewn to complete the center medallion.

Center medallion assembly

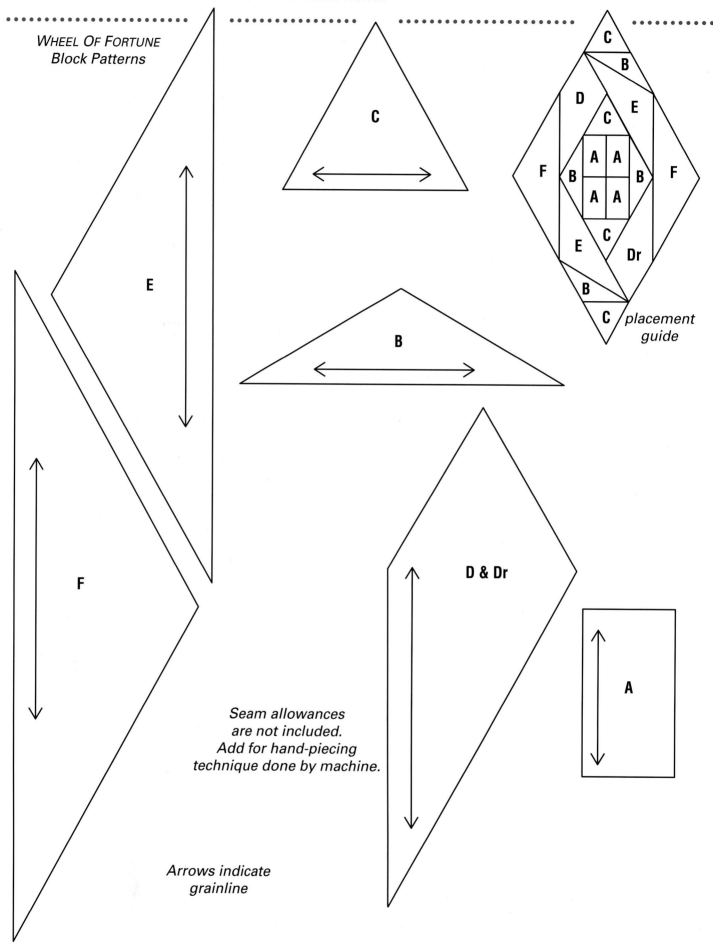

WHEEL OF FORTUNE
Block Patterns

C

E

F

B

C

D & Dr

placement
guide

A

*Seam allowances
are not included.
Add for hand-piecing
technique done by machine.*

*Arrows indicate
grainline*

Different design and color options for the center medallion

Ann Feitelson

Montague, Massachusetts

MEET THE QUILTER

I loved the 1971 Whitney Museum exhibit, Abstract Design in American Quilts. It was the first time quilts were on the walls of an art museum. I saw the exhibit with my mother, who had taught me about color, pattern, sewing, knitting, weaving, and needlepoint. She had great taste and no hesitation about tackling the most challenging projects. My mother didn't quilt, but she had bought a few treasured quilts, which I slept under as a child. So, from the outset, I knew of quilts both as comfort and as dazzling abstract art.

I majored in art in college. The summer after I graduated in 1972, while living on a commune, I made a quilt. I sewed much of it by hand and finished it on my mother's Singer®. That fall, I went to art school in New York City and ultimately received a master's degree in painting and went on to teach painting and drawing at two colleges. I worked seriously painting landscapes and still lifes for about 10 years.

In 1985, while I was working for a public art project, One Percent for Art, Michael James submitted slides of his work for consideration. I loved his work and invited him to give a presentation. I met him then, and his work remains an important inspiration to me.

... any block, any color, or any pattern can be a vehicle for passionate, exciting color, or for an interesting composition. It is color and shape and the dynamic forces they create that carry meaning.

Ann's photo by Bruce Kushnick

One Thing Leads to Another

60" x 60"

In 1990, I became fascinated with Fair Isle knitting so I went to Shetland to study it. I made friends with knitters there and subsequently made four more trips to Shetland. I wrote *The Art of Fair Isle Knitting* (Interweave Press, 1996), which featured sweaters of my own design and a history of Fair Isle knitting. I also taught knitting around the country.

While I was knitting Fair Isle sweaters, I took three paint-and-paper classes with Michael James on color and design, thinking they could be useful for my knitting. Then I took a fourth class with him in 1999 – this time using fabric – and I have been quilting since then.

INSPIRATION AND DESIGN

Through all these phases of my interest in art, my real passion has been color. I also love to be challenged and to learn new things. I made ONE THING LEADS TO ANOTHER specifically for this contest. The Monkey Wrench block didn't inspire me initially. The first few blocks I made seemed boring, but any block, or any pattern can be a vehicle for passionate, exciting color or for an interesting composition. It is color and shape and the dynamic forces they create that carry meaning. A line can zing or plod. A blue can be lyrical or depressing.

I found color inspiration in the Aurora collection fabrics by RJR. They shade very gradually, for example, from lovely pale greens to turquoises to blues to purples across 44". I put a half dozen half-yard pieces of these fabrics in several colorways on my design wall and worked with and against those colors to create a composition. I used the shaded fabrics as a substructure like an underpainting.

I also used the shaded fabrics to build a critical mass of blocks. I then removed the underlayer of fabrics and began to adjust the quilt's composition, looking for large simple shapes. I like simple compositions, simple blocks, and simple quilting, but not simple color. I like complex, shifting, vibrant color and the richness of low-contrast colors. I use little fabric with high value contrast. I like blocks in which the colors are so close that you can hardly see the piecing.

I tend to need only small bits of fabric and like having an extensive palette, so I rely on subscriptions to 10" squares and fat sixteenths rather than buying yardage. I like getting fabric in the mail that I wouldn't have chosen in a store. It gives me a small dissent thrill to use something I don't like.

As for the title, ONE THING LEADS TO ANOTHER, I refer to the bizarre coincidences and trials of life. Seemingly small incidents can have enormous repercussions. An ordinary day and a year flow seamlessly, yet major things are different from one year to the next. You don't wind up where you start. Similarly, color flows closely in many places yet arrives somewhere dramatically surprising. I create this flow in some places by using the same fabric in the inner triangles of one block and in the outer triangles of the neighboring block. Then the inner triangles of the second block are in the outer triangles of a third block, and so on.

While the blocks may be progressing in a sequence of colors in one direction, the centers may be progressing in a sequence of colors in another direction. A three-color block is infinitely more exciting than a two-color block. It seems that the mind can juggle or follow two colors relatively easily, but when you add a third color progression, you stop being able to follow simultaneous "conversations." Things fall apart; the eye gets lost; it wanders and jumps. Even though my color decisions were in some way logical, there is an element of the absurd, too. I use things I don't like, I allow the piecing to crop a print so that the seams are obscured, and I make the blocks almost impossible to discern.

I rarely make preparatory drawing or sketches because I compose as I go along. I made about half again as many blocks as are in the final quilt. They were edited out during the process of refin-

ing the color. I have enough of those for another quilt. Leftovers are like sourdough; they pave the way for the next quilt.

BATIK BINDING

Rather than use French double-fold binding, I used a single thickness of binding, which is flatter. In knitting, it is a given that the edges flare, so you always draw the edge in slightly by using fewer stitches or a smaller needle and tighter gauge. I transferred this rule to quilt edges and find that my bindings lie flat if they are slightly smaller than the quilt. For every 4" along the edge, I cut long grain binding of taut batiks $\frac{1}{16}$" shorter and match it to 4" block segments.

Detail from ONE THING LEADS TO ANOTHER

Laura Fogg

Ukiah, California

MEET THE QUILTER

I guess it's time to quit telling people that I am a new quilter. I've been doing this for six years now, and have gotten over the shakes experienced early on. Then, I was intimidated by producing in cloth what my mind's eye could see so clearly. Now, fabric is my natural medium and each piece is started with a feeling of excitement and anticipation of success.

It's taken me most of my life to discover fabric as an art medium. Fabric was used for making clothes, which I did with a considerable amount of enthusiasm during high school. I kept sewing clothes while my children were young enough to appreciate the unique made-at-home look, then branched out into wild and fanciful stuffed animals when the kids decided they preferred Mervyn's to Mom's for their apparel. The animals were fun, but I never got passionate about them.

Throughout my education, from kindergarten to graduate school, I took every art class that fit into my schedule. I happily messed around with the usual array of paints and pencils, ceramics, and collage objects, but knew in my gut that the right road had not been found. Always attracted to the texture and movement of textiles, I tried knitting, embroidery, needlepoint, and weaving, but found them to be painfully slow and lacking spontaneity in the creation process. I settled on mural painting, which gave me practice creating large and dynamic landscape compositions.

I galloped back to the ship and headed to my makeshift studio. While the other passengers were streaming up the gangway with their tired spouses and huge bags of Skagway purchases, I was spreading out my fabrics and attacking them with scissors.

The white flower heads were made from chenille yarn. With two strands together for the greatest amount of loft manageable, I wrapped the yarn three times around the tip of my sewing scissors and slipped the resulting wad in place on the quilt (fig. 3). Then, the whole thing was smashed under the stippling foot and sewn around in little circles to hold it down. I used a green variegated thread to achieve some color depth, and didn't worry about being neat. Nothing in nature is neat. Without cutting the yarn, I made another wad similar to the previous one, and repeated this process until each flower looked full and artistically balanced.

Fig. 2. Attaching leaves to the surface

Fig. 3. Sewing chenille yarn

Karen Griska

Nashville, Tennessee

MEET THE QUILTER

I don't think I have ever made a quilt from a pattern. That would not be fun for me. My best quilts are the ones that are not planned in advance, but start with an idea and develop along the way.

Since 1999, I have enjoyed some aspect of quilting almost every day and have made about 200 quilts since my first at age 13. One wall of my studio is covered with a large piece of flannel, about 80" x 100". This generous width allows room for pieces to remain in view until they have a home in a quilt.

I love the design process. The delight of discoveries, the process of handling fabrics and putting them all together, and a finished product that is sometimes more stunning than I imagined, are what fuel my passion for quilting.

Years ago, I started keeping a notebook with pictures taken from calendars, books, and magazines of my favorite quilts. Among the massive mix, I started to notice some common threads. I like quilts that have many different fabrics, small pieces, and bright colors in unusual combinations. Bold designs and some improvisation or surprise catch my eye. Among my favorites are crazy quilts, antique quilts, and Amish-style quilts. Many enjoyable hours have been spent studying this notebook.

The delight of discoveries, the process of handling fabrics and putting them all together, and a finished product that is sometimes more stunning than I imagined, are what fuel my passion for quilting.

Quartet In Mosaic

59" x 60"

Other important sources of inspiration are picture books of antique quilts, particularly the state quilt survey books. I seem to have an endless supply of quilt ideas and each quilt I make generates even more.

I was a hermit quilter until joining the Cumberland Valley Quilter's Guild. Now I enjoy sharing my passion for quilting with other enthusiastic quilters. This is a wonderful source of friendship and encouragement.

It is such an honor to have a quilt exhibited at the Museum of the American Quilter's Society. I hope to inspire and encourage quilters to have more fun making unique quilts with their hearts rather than with patterns.

INSPIRATION AND DESIGN

This contest challenged me to stretch beyond what I have done before, to come up with a truly innovative approach to the Monkey Wrench. I've always liked this block, but never really pondered it before.

Originally, I wanted to try for an Amish look with a bold design in an unusual solid-color combination. I planned to embellish the entire quilt with mosaic tiles. After studying pictures of mosaics and experimenting with this style in quilting, I see many creative and beautiful ways mosaic will be part of my quilting in the future.

Color selection was easy. At the fabric store, possible combinations were arranged on the floor. I wanted a dark but not black fabric, and a light but not white fabric. I needed a color that would sing pretty loud and make it all work. Finally, the trio had to be a little strange; not a combination you see all

the time. The choice was made: dark plum, light gold, and red. You just can't go wrong with red.

This quilt was designed as I went along. I could never have come up with this design in my mind. My original concept of one very large Monkey Wrench was changed to four fairly large blocks. This was less intense and, fortunately, decided before the fabric was cut.

Once the blocks were made, the background was filled with broken tiles of dark plum, ironed on with fusible web. I really like the high contrast here and was thrilled with the red center squares. This classic element in many traditional Log Cabin quilts was right at home here. The red squares called for some red sashing of the same width.

At this point, restraint became the key. I originally planned to mosaic the entire quilt, but that proved to be much too busy. The Monkey Wrenches looked cleaner without mosaic. The same was true for the red sashing. Another change came when the wide dark plum border was auditioned on the design wall. Suddenly, the Monkey Wrenches looked like background and the quilt became dark. The border, then, had to be light gold.

The ironed-on sawtooth triangles in the border were inspired by the half-square triangles in the Monkey Wrenches. This made the blocks stand out nicely. The wavy, vertical machine-quilting lines were made with smoke-colored monofilament thread, so as to make them quietly visible in the light gold areas, but not shiny in the Monkey Wrench or red areas.

The finished quilt is simple and bold, yet intricate. The process of applying the mosaic tiles was relaxing. With no fussing or agonizing, most pieces were placed "as is" and some were custom cut.

MOSAIC TILES

When I start a quilt, it is much easier to not pre-determine the final size and try to calculate the dimensions of all the parts. Instead, I make blocks or units of a pleasing size. Generally, I like small pieces and keep building until it looks right. Occasionally, I end up with a quilt much bigger than expected.

In a mosaic quilt, the pieced or whole-cloth top can be the background, or the grout, for the quilt design. It is good to experiment with tiles of different color, value, and size. Tiles made of a variety of fabrics, including some from printed fabrics, add interest and excitement. Fabrics that look like china plates are fun to use in mosaic.

To make the tiles, apply fusible web to the wrong side of the fabric with a dry iron, according to the instructions on the package. With the paper side up, draw 1" wide strips, then cut along the lines with sharp scissors. The line will be less straight than a rotary-cut line, but will produce a more charming appearance. Keep the paper in place while cutting because the stiffness will make the long line easier to cut. Once the strips are cut,

remove the paper and randomly cut tiles with scissors. Avoid cutting long, skinny points because these may curl or peel off. I cut the tiles onto a tray so they are easy to move without handling too much. This keeps the edges from fraying.

Lay the tiles in a pleasing arrangement on the quilt top and secure them with a steam iron. Working a small area at a time reduces the risk of messing up your arrangement. Some tiles will need to be custom cut, which gets easier with practice. Precision is not an important objective here. When you see mosaic work in the future, notice the degree of precision, or lack thereof, and the resulting effect.

During the machine-quilting process, I try to make contact with all the mosaic pieces for greater security. The tiles seem to adhere just fine without hand or machine appliqué around the edge of each little piece.

Mosaic would probably not be a good choice for a utility quilt. This is art, and we don't expect all art to be machine washable. Mosaic quilts are more like crazy quilts or novelty quilts in this regard.

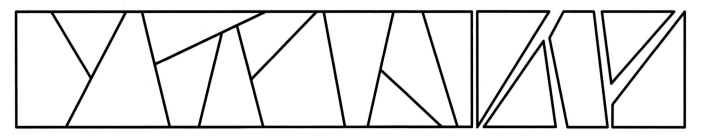

Cutting mosaic tiles from fabric strips. Avoid cutting long, skinny points because these may curl or peel off.

Mary Ann Herndon

Spring, Texas

MEET THE QUILTER

Art, in almost any form, has always been a major focus for me. Experimenting with painting, fabric-related crafts, and most recently, fused glass, has filled any free hours I've had.

The time I devoted to any purely creative endeavors had been limited by raising three children, who are now grown, and working 30 years as a teacher, librarian, and library director for a school district. Now that I'm retired, I find that all my ideas for quilt designs could not possibly be completed, even in several lifetimes. Therefore, I'm trying to be a little more selective in the projects started and completed.

My inspiration comes from seeing the works of other quilters, but I find that more original ideas come from viewing other art forms such as paintings, illustrative art, children's book illustrations, and glass art. All my quilts until now have been hand quilted and hand drafted. If I expect to finish even a fraction of the pieces I have planned, machine quilting and the computer will need to be conquered.

My previous experience with machine quilting has been a disaster, but I hope practice helps. It's taking time for that practice! The same goes for the computer. I can e-mail,

A great design with poor color can destroy a quilt's impact, while wonderful colors with a mediocre design can sometimes result in a "wow" quilt.

75½" x 67"

browse, and search, but learning a quilt design program has taken more time than I've been willing to give. I now have four updates for a quilt program that has never been taken out of the box.

For the most part, the quilts I make are intended for competitions. Like most quilters, I started making traditional quilts and learning the basics. Replicating patterns by others helped me learn techniques and processes. I continue to take classes from teachers whose quilts I admire, but usually with the intention of using some of their techniques to inspire original creations. Making a quilt with 25 blocks that are all the same never did really seem much fun, but trying to twist and turn a traditional block into an innovative art piece inspires me.

The overall impact of a quilt is the most important aspect of the piece to me. The concept of a quilt is interesting after the fact, but the initial view of a quilt that makes you catch your breath and say "wow" is very important. Fabric and design are so closely related when I start a piece, that it's hard to say which comes first. A great design with poor color can destroy a quilt's impact, while wonderful colors with a mediocre design can sometimes result in a "wow" quilt.

INSPIRATION AND DESIGN

The museum contest and a black fabric with metallic print provided the inspiration for RAZZLE DAZZLE. I have entered this contest in the past and really enjoyed the challenge. The quilt's design was my first concern because I knew an innovative twist to the traditional Monkey Wrench pattern had to be the focus.

I decided to redraft the pattern into a diamond shape rather than a square and paper piece it. To plan the setting, the diamonds were photocopied with the redrafted Monkey Wrench colored in black and white in varying positions. The blocks were cut out and positioned in several settings. I wanted a setting that resulted in a radiating pattern rather than a series of separate blocks.

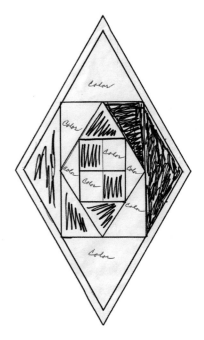

Mary Ann's original sketch for RAZZLE DAZZLE

Once a pattern was chosen for the diamonds, it was not hard to choose fabrics. With the metallic print already purchased, a trip to several quilt shops resulted in a shaded material. I love shaded fabric because it provides an effect that is harder to achieve with gradated separate pieces.

The next step was to decide the shading sequence from the middle to the outside. To do this, I placed tracing paper over my mock-up and colored some scenarios. A yellow-orange-fuchsia-orange color scheme was chosen.

After these major decisions, I enlarged the diamond to the size calculated for the quilt and made enough photocopies for the plan. Then, notes on each diamond were made to indicate colors, because paper piecing a radiating pattern that gradually changes colors can get confusing.

For the border, I intended to continue the black metallic background. After pinning it on my design wall and trying both the black and a shaded border, the shaded border seemed more striking. I really wanted it wider but didn't have enough fabric left.

I think this quilt's design could be interesting with many other color choices. Some wonderful kaleidoscopic patterns could be incorporated with selective cutting for the diamond points. When the quilt comes back to me after the exhibit, I will try to add more quilting because time simply ran out on me, but what else is new. A lack of time for most quilters is rather universal. "So many quilts, so little time."

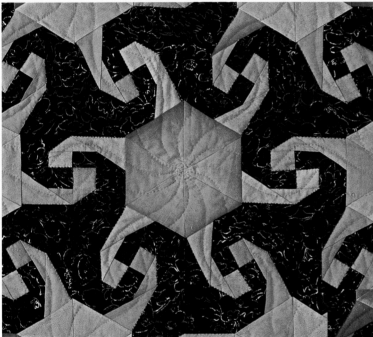

Details from RAZZLE DAZZLE

Chris Lynn Kirsch & Sharon Rotz

Oconomowoc, Wisconsin   Mosinee, Wisconsin

We began sketching
monkeys, and all too soon,
they were hooking up
together and running
with wrenches.

MEET THE QUILTERS

Chris Lynn Kirsch:

From childhood, I have loved the joy of creating and working with fabric. After moving to a new area in 1987, I was talked into taking a quilt class by my sister-in-law. I really did not want to learn to quilt, but felt it would be a good way to meet people. My sister-in-law never finished her quilt and I became an addict! I collected books and patterns and stitched every traditional style of quilt available.

After a while, I wanted to create original designs, but quickly decided I couldn't without a background in art. With a bit of encouragement from friends and teachers, I took the plunge and a few of my first original pieces were ribbon winners. This was inspiring and has led me into the exciting world of art quilts.

I began teaching quiltmaking and have found that guiding students to create their own work is very gratifying. I enjoy entering competitions, and my award-winning quilts have been exhibited worldwide. This is my third quilt accepted into the Museum of the American Quilter's Society contest.

Five years ago, I was invited to teach at a quilting retreat and assigned to share a room with a teacher whom I had never met. In no time, I discovered Sharon had a whacky sense of humor and an amazing talent for workmanship

Two Friends Monkeying Around

59" x 59"

and creativity. We giggled until late into the night and a wonderful friendship was born. We are blessed by our ability to work well together, which has caused us to stretch our creativity and workmanship.

Sharon Rotz: An early interest in fabrics and design led me to a degree in home economics education. Early job opportunities found me working under a professional tailor and in the ready-made industry. Relocation and a young family led to a home-based business, fabricating draperies and unique home accessories.

After several years of interior decorating, I met my first quilters and my sewing machine and I were drawn in a new direction. My lifetime collection of scraps did not include the appropriate fabrics for quilting and were gradually discarded. Other than that, it was a fast and easy transition into the world of rotary cutters and ¼" seam allowances.

My enthusiasm for quilting led me to quilt shows, where I began to exhibit my own work. Years of professional-quality sewing led to prize-winning quilts, venues in juried shows, and having my work included in traveling exhibits. With an education background, teaching was a natural progression. Motivating quilters is never a problem and it is wonderfully rewarding to help others develop their talents.

Through my quilts, I push the limits on color and attempt to break out of the expected. I am becoming more attracted to art quilts and the design opportunities they present. My once discarded stash of non-quilting fabrics is being replenished as I venture from the traditional, although I still admire the beauty and workmanship of traditional quilts and like to retain some elements of traditional quilting in my work.

Although I like to plan for things, I've found the unexpected happenings of my life are the most enriching. One of these unexpected blessings was meeting Chris. She is an innovative quilter, inspiring others with her strong faith and passion for quilting. We both respect each other's abilities and are in tune with our reactions, which is a key to working together. We both contribute equally and try our best, not only for self-satisfaction, but more importantly, for each other. And how could we not mention the sharing of a little silliness.

Inspiration & Design

Chris Lynn Kirsch: This past August, we had a sleepover at Sharon's home. I brought along a plan for a telescoping design of the simple Monkey Wrench block, along with a few yards of a wonderful black hand-dyed fabric. Staring at it for a while, we were not enthused. We threw other fabrics into the mix and once the red fabrics were chosen, Two Friends Monkeying Around seemed to almost make itself. We both share a Christian faith and feel there was something bigger at work here for things to have gone so well.

We began cutting and stitching and everything fit perfectly without ever comparing seam allowances. By the time we went to bed, the top was pieced. The following morning we brainstormed quilting ideas. The design was so simple that the quilting had to make it special.

The color scheme had an oriental feel, so Sharon pulled out some oriental design books and we realized that many of the designs involved circles of intertwining vines and flowers. We began sketching monkeys, and all too soon, they were hooking up together and running with wrenches.

An initial circle was marked, then it was time for me to head home. I took the quilt top and started with trapunto and stippling around the monkeys in that ring. Because we live four hours apart, the rest would need to be done via mail. The quilt was returned to Sharon and she continued designing, marking, and quilting. It went back and forth until the quilt was finished.

Sharon Rotz: When Chris showed me her simple Monkey Wrench design, I was less than impressed. I had envisioned appliquéd monkeys with wrenches climbing all over a network of pipes. The beauty of working with a partner is that bizarre ideas are tempered with more rational thought and discussion. We both loved the drama of a black-and-red color scheme and the simplicity of the design would lead to exploring fabulous ideas for machine quilting.

We both wanted the quilt to have a strong visual effect, yet draw you in with interesting details. This was accomplished with the large, dramatic blocks, followed by the circular design of the quilting, and finally noting the monkey shapes and Monkey Wrench block motifs. I finally got my monkeys with wrenches!

MAKING OVERSIZED BLOCKS

Chris Lynn Kirsch: One of the first problems Sharon and I encountered in this project was constructing the corner half-square triangles, which measure 22¾" square. It is not necessary to have a ruler as large as the block, but it is helpful to have a cutting mat larger than the block. An excellent feature in a mat is a 1" grid with numbers on the outside of the grid so fabric does not cover them when aligned with the zero.

To illustrate our method for cutting the triangles, the following instructions are for cutting two squares at 21" for 19½" finished-size blocks. This measurement

comes from adding a ⅞" half-square triangle seam allowance to the finished size, then adding extra. Due to the large block size, the squares are cut slightly larger than necessary and trimmed to the required size.

1. Fold one fabric selvage to selvage and square it along one edge with a cut perpendicular to the fold. Lay the cut edge along the zero line on the cutting mat and place the ruler along the 21" line. Cut along the ruler perpendicular to the fold (fig. 1).

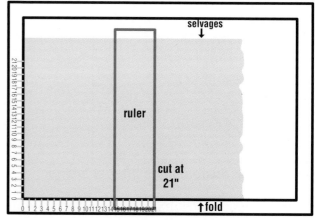

Fig. 1. Cut at 21", perpendicular to the fold.

2. Turn this piece a quarter turn, leaving it doubled, and cut along a ruler to trim the selvages. Lay this new cut along the zero line, keeping both layers even, and cut the bulk off at 21" (fig. 2).

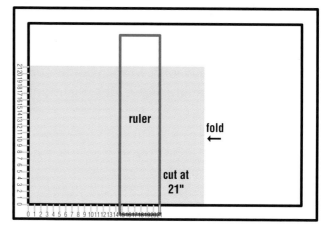

Fig. 2. Cut once again at 21".

3. Repeat steps 1 and 2 for the contrasting fabric. Draw a diagonal line along the wrong side of each lighter square. Layer a light square with a contrasting square, right sides together, and pin along the diagonal line.

4. Stitch ¼" on each side of the diagonal line (fig. 3). Cut on the line and press the seam allowances to the dark fabric.

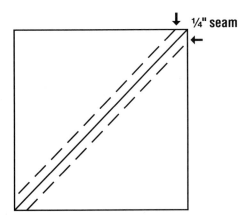

Fig. 3. Cut the diagonal line after stitching.

This yields four half-square triangle blocks which are larger than 20". Square these blocks precisely, making sure the diagonal runs exactly from corner to corner in the finished blocks.

COMBINING TECHNOLOGY AND CUT-OUT DOLLS

Sharon Rotz: The simplicity of our design gave us the opportunity to explore new directions in creative quilting. To balance the straight lines of the piecing, we both thought curves. We loved the beauty of the flowing oriental circular designs. I still liked the monkeys with wrenches theme, and why not. Originally an appliqué idea, the monkeys became our quilting focus. We began sketching, and soon the oriental-inspired circles of vines and flowers became visions of monkeys intertwining and running with wrenches.

Even with limited drawing abilities, we managed to produce several recognizable monkeys. Because we like laying out the shapes and arranging them on the actual quilt, we took our drawings to the computer scanner where we enlarged and reduced them to scale. Even those with limited computer expertise can master this approach. Draw or trace your shape with a strong black line, such as a permanent marker. This is especially important if you reduce your drawing. Scan a preview of your drawing. Adjust the selection area to fit the size of your shape and change the output dimensions to fit the space on your quilt. We tried a few sizes to get the best fit as we overlapped and chained our shapes into an interesting design.

We could have used our computer to print several copies of each monkey, but remembering the childhood joy of cutting paper dolls, we simply stapled the pattern to a stack of paper and cut out monkeys. Soon they were everywhere and in all sizes.

We wanted to create that flowing circular effect so the monkey shapes would be noticed only on close inspection. Chris came up with a wonderful plan and our initial circle was marked.

The straight angular lines of the block proved to be the perfect foil for the curving monkeys. The block motif, reducing in size, spiraled into the center, complementing the telescoping Monkey Wrench piecing. Quilting was done in metallic, rayon, and variegated threads. Trapunto surrounded with stippling added extra relief to our dominant monkey circle.

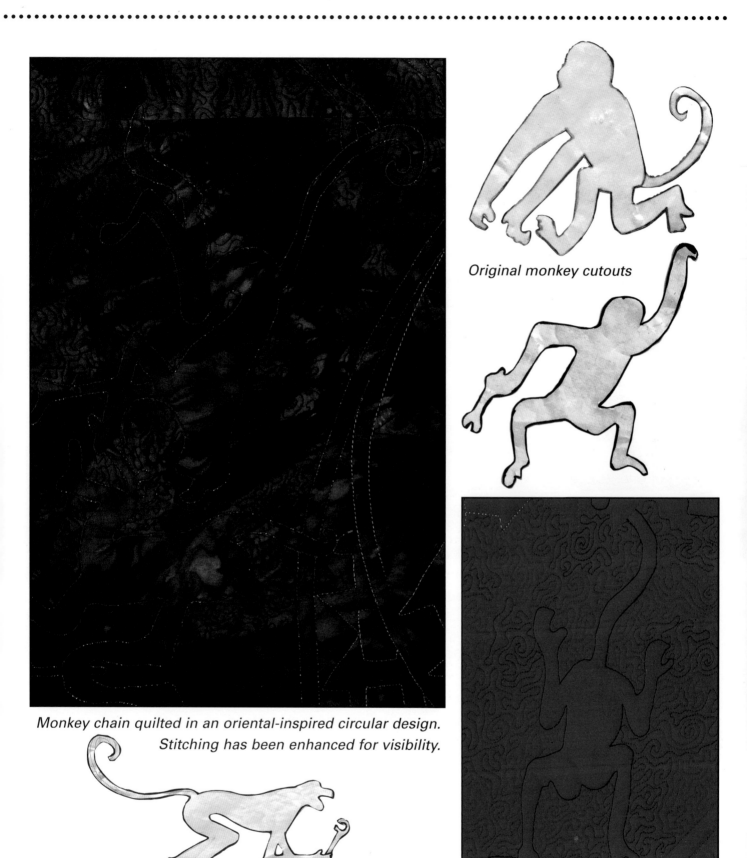

Original monkey cutouts

Monkey chain quilted in an oriental-inspired circular design. Stitching has been enhanced for visibility.

Quilted monkey holding a wrench

Marlene Silha Martin

Danville, Kentucky

MEET THE QUILTER

I began quilting about four years ago, but have sewn for as many years as I can remember. My mother, Daphne Silha, is an excellent quilter and has quilted for some time. Never being able to sit still long enough to hand quilt, I didn't really quilt until later in life.

After moving to Kentucky from Texas, I started making jackets. When a new quilt shop opened, I took a couple of jackets to show the owner, but she was never there. However, Leslie Taylor, who was running the store, asked me to join an evening quilt group. She explained that I could work on jackets while others quilted.

The group came up with a terrific idea for making quilts from preprinted panels. I thought this looked fun and tried one. The quilt seemed easy, even though my base blocks were all different sizes. To this day, my dogs love their quilt with whole, half, and quarter blocks. The quilt's only saving grace was that it arrived square.

My first quilting class was shortly after that with David Walker. I remember one exercise in which we were supposed to represent ourselves. Being a psychologist, I was under the impression we were to get in touch with our inner child. I was laughing and having a wonderful time. When we shared our pictures, mine looked like a cave painting with yarn and threads everywhere as part of the design. Everyone else, including my 80-year-old mother, had a design worthy of an art exhibit.

I felt like the monkey in the old saying, "Monkey see, monkey do." I strongly identify with the monkey in my quilt, contemplating a tool and wondering if it is correct for the job.

Is This a Monkey Wrench?

53" x 62½"

From there, my mother and I began frequenting sewing and quilt shows. Quilting became a special way for the two of us to share something we both love and to have special time together. My supportive husband, Bob, says that living with me since I began quilting is like living with a large dog that sheds thread.

I love trying new ideas and techniques. Having worked for years in the computer field, I feel at home with quilt design software. Designing on the computer, I can make 20 or 30 quilts in one night.

This quilt was inspired by all the people who fix our sewing machines and keep us sewing. I have found that people are the true inspiration for my quilts. My heart is touched by the joys and challenges we all face in a world that is becoming more complex, even at the level of the simple sewing machine.

INSPIRATION AND DESIGN

I was drawn to this competition by the block title, Monkey Wrench. It seemed to have numerous fun design possibilities. The one thing I was sure about was that my design would include a monkey with a wrench.

While designing this quilt, I had begun training to repair sewing machines. Although my father was a mechanical engineer, I never paid much attention to the names of his various tools. Fortunately, my teacher, Kevin Charles, patiently answered my many questions on the tools of the trade. Trying to duplicate exactly what he was doing, I felt like the monkey in the old saying, "Monkey see, monkey do." I strongly identified with the monkey in my quilt, as I would contemplate a tool and wonder if it were correct for the job.

After several iterations during design, I noticed that curving certain sections of the block changed the look from a monkey wrench to a standard wrench. I added blocks to the pattern and changed colors to make the quilt look like there were multiple wrenches. Still, the viewer could see the original Monkey Wrench block. Although one could see that this was a variation, it no longer looked like the traditional block, hence the title, IS THIS A MONKEY WRENCH?

CONSTRUCTING THE QUILT

With quilt design software, I played with block variations. After designing the block, I placed it in a setting to look for secondary patterns.

I always design in color on the computer, but print blocks and quilt designs in shades of black and white. I have found that knowing the design and color values frees me to play with color in fabric. For instance, once I started to work in fabric, I changed the colors in the block three times before settling on a color scheme.

My color choices are influenced by my sewing background in clothing and I tend to use similar values. In this quilt, a combination of cotton batiks and commercial hand-painted fabric is used. As blocks are pieced, they are added to the design wall. If a block is not working, I simply put it aside and do another one. The discarded blocks go to charity quilts.

Once this quilt was designed, I began piecing from the black and white design. While adding to the design wall, I discovered that the border was not working. It was redesigned to add visual interest and reinterpret the block. Then, I added the bolts along with the other Monkey Wrench blocks.

The monkey itself was drawn, then fused to muslin, and appliquéd to the quilt with free-hand stitching after the quilting was complete. I left the monkey as a representation rather than an exact likeness. I love eyelash trim and it seemed perfect for the hair around the monkey's face. Couching along and on the quilt border helped to add further texture. The quilt was machine pieced and quilted on my home sewing machine, primarily with free-motion quilting.

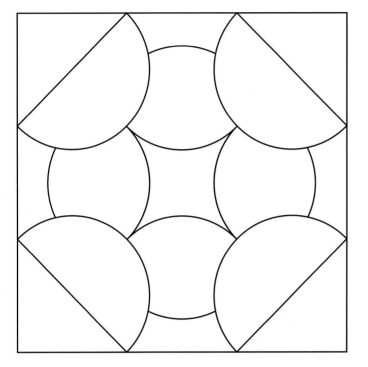

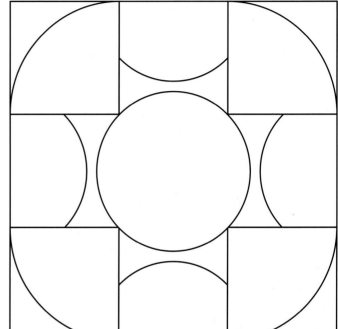

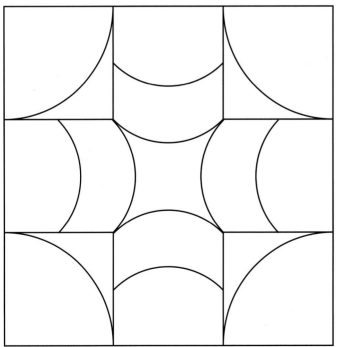

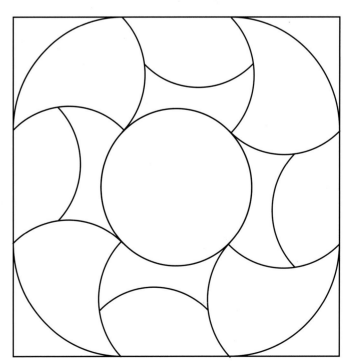

Marlene's initial sketches

Maurine Roy

Edmonds, Washington

MEET THE QUILTER

My first attempt at quilting was in 1990 when I took a six-month appliqué and hand quilting class from Nancy Ann Twelker. We made five blocks in five months, and the settings and borders in the sixth month. I became obsessed with blocks, and since that time, have finished over 200 quilts.

I have hand quilted several large quilts and wallhangings, but most of my work is machine quilted. I took several classes from Maurine Noble on machine quilting and decorative threads. She is my greatest inspiration.

I have taken advantage of the many wonderful teachers and classes offered through Quilting by the Sound and through my quilt guild, which includes Caryl Bryer Fallert, David Walker, Nancy Crow, Laura Carter Woods, Barbara Olson, Paula Nadlestern, Lee Hackman, Elizabeth Busch, Judy Dales, Margaret Miller, Katie Pasquini, Libby Lehman, and many others.

I am fortunate to live in the Pacific Northwest. The area seems to draw top teachers from around the world. I attend as many classes and workshops as possible to learn new techniques and improve my work. This has given me the ability to technically achieve any design idea I may have.

I enjoy the challenge of trying new ideas and concepts in design. Most of my art quilts are original designs. Some ideas come easy and turn into quilts quickly, while others

Quilting is an amazing art form. Once you step into the world of quilting, you find there are no limitations on your creativity or your depth of feelings.

Shall We Dance?

50" x 50"

have to simmer awhile before the idea becomes clear enough to work on. So far, I have not had too many problems running out of ideas, but have known the panic of hitting a dry spell.

My one strict rule is to finish every quilt top I make. If I get three or four quilt tops finished, I always stop and quilt them. Sometimes, it is hard to keep up with all my ideas. Many quilts reflect my experiences and feelings. I have made a few therapy quilts. Somehow, working with the texture and color of fabric helps release and sooth emotions. Quilting is an amazing art form. Once you step into the world of quilting, you find there are no limitations on your creativity or your depth of feelings.

My work has been published in numerous books and magazines. I was the featured artist at the LaConner Quilt Museum for two months with my show, A Journey Thru Possibilities. I won a gold award from the International Quilt Show in Osaka, Japan. I have also won awards from the American Quilter's Society Quilt Show, the International Quilt Festival, the Pacific International Quilt Show, and the Pacific Northwest Quiltfest.

INSPIRATION AND DESIGN

I have always wanted to make a Snail's Trail quilt, but never found the time. Upon accepting this challenge, I made quite a few blocks with different fabrics, looking for inspiration. Finally, I decided on a black background with my hand-dyed fabrics. I made several blocks, some with the pattern reversed, then played with them until a pattern emerged.

As I randomly placed the blocks on my wall, I noticed that the blue-green gradation formed a square. This became my starting point. As the blues formed a square, so did the red gradation. The dark blue triangle on the block was not vivid

enough and got lost, so it was substituted with a commmercial fabric to put some pizazz in the quilt. With this, the square seemed to pop out.

I made a sketch of the setting, estimated that approximately 40 blocks would be needed, and started sewing the blocks, half of them reversed. I used a paper-piecing technique, substituting freezer paper with a very fine, soft interfacing that could be left in. Because I have arthritis in my thumbs, it is painful to remove the freezer paper and this soft interfacing works wonderfully well.

The fun and the challenge were playing with the regular and reverse blocks to bring out the pattern envisioned. The tricky part was figuring out which way the tails would face. The center seemed to work better with the tails all in the same direction, giving it more movement.

My quilt was designed without much thought to the border. I experimented with several borders, and believe this one brings the whole quilt together. With the fuchsia triangle from the Snail's Trail

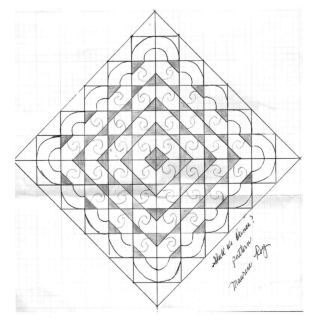

Maurine's initial sketch

block as the start, I used four gradations from red to yellow, then four yellow to red to complete one border block.

I enjoyed making this quilt and became rather obsessed with the placement of the blocks. I couldn't leave it alone, and spent much time between total frustration and pleasure with the way it was developing. When it was finished and hanging in the living room, I imagined a magical evening with dancers twirling around a dance floor, hence the name, SHALL WE DANCE?

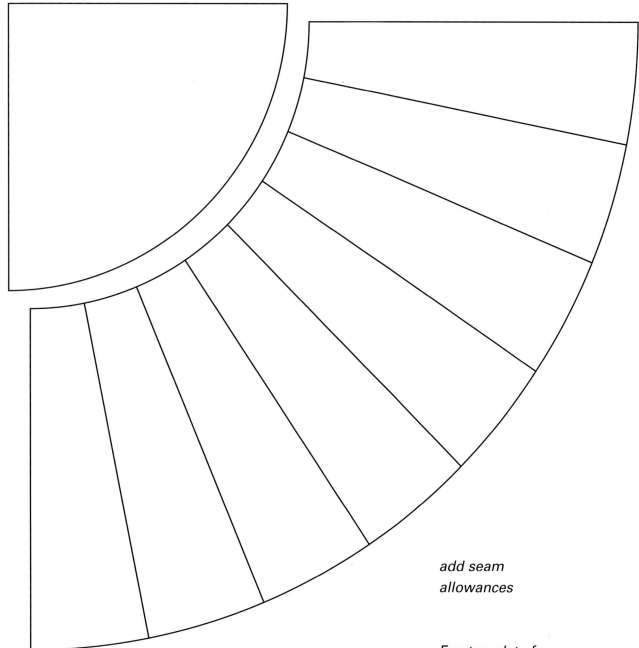

add seam allowances

Fan template for SHALL WE DANCE? border

Lucy Silliman

Fort Scott, Kansas

MEET THE QUILTER

My philosophy is to do something on a quilt to make it uniquely different from all the millions of others that went before. After learning sewing skills on traditional patterns, I have branched out by making my own design statement. This quilt is a glance back to tradition. The contest was appealing because the Monkey Wrench pattern makes such a visual statement.

Quilting offers me a deep sense of satisfaction to experiment with new ideas. It is important to keep thinking and growing. With quilting, there is always a new way to solve problems and a new challenge. While there is nothing really new in working on an old design favorite, there is a new twist or variation. That's why the quilts in a contest such as this are so enjoyable. There are infinite variations.

My present work is going in a new direction. I have always made very large pieces. Now, I'm experimenting with painting much of my own fabric and making small, intimate pieces. What does the future of my quiltmaking hold? That's the best part – I never know!

I have often claimed that I would never make a quilt a certain way, only to discover that my journey may lead in that direction. Life is always changing and we must forever change and grow. With fabric and thread, we can each be individuals working in our own unique

The decor of my house is a mixture of antiques and contemporary art, so why not my quilt. I've always loved blending things that at first might not seem compatible.

Lucy's photo by Gary Palmer, Captured Images, Fort Scott, Kansas

Stripes, Dots & Friends

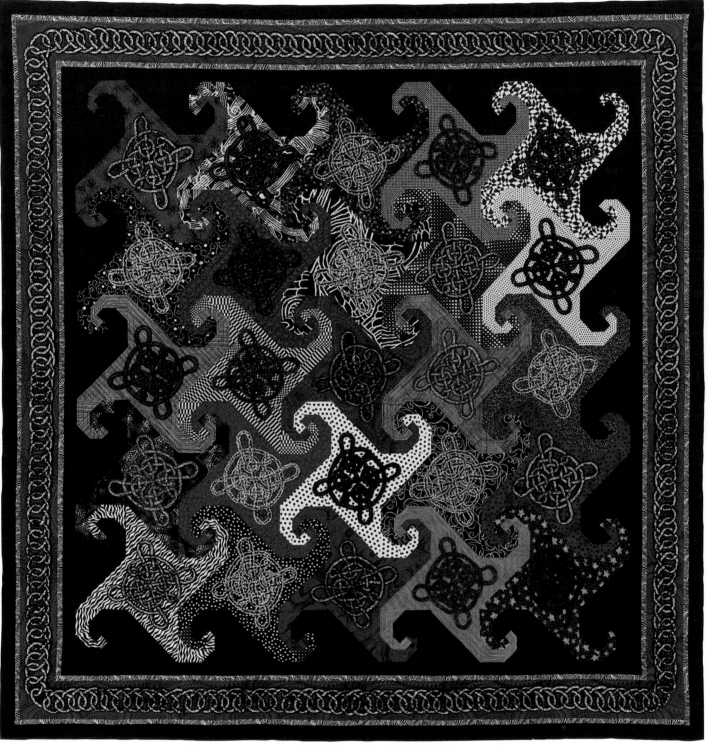

81" x 81"

styles. I love seeing what others do with the same gem of an idea with which I begin. Isn't it wonderful that we are all on the path of quiltmaking, but each at our own station? We will never reach the end because there is always the next project. That's the beauty of it all!

INSPIRATION AND DESIGN

The Monkey Wrench pattern, or Snail's Trail as it is known in most of Kansas, has always been an intriguing design. The twists and turns look complicated, but it is actually a simple block based on the Square-in-a-Square pattern. Only the arrangement of fabrics changes it from a static block to a design in which the quiltmaker can monkey around.

STRIPES, DOTS & FRIENDS is really a straightforward interpretation of the pattern. I began by looking for favorites in my fabric stash. As I age, I've decided that no one else will want all of my many beloved, unusual fabrics. Therefore, my motto has become to "use the best first," with no fabric being too beautiful or valuable to cut. I worked hard shopping for all of these beauties and delight in the eye candy they create.

Cutting and experimenting with the colors is the most fun of all. Black and white with a huge infusion of red is a very graphic color combination. The starkness of the black and white is quickly offset by the vibrancy of the hot red.

To make the design even more graphic, why not add stripes and dots? Then, the challenge begins because there are all sorts of different stripes. The same can be said for dots. There are regular, evenly spaced dots, but the ones I like best are the mavericks that aren't quite round or not what a dictionary would describe as a dot. I added a few friends that didn't quite fit either of the two descriptions, stripe or dot. My favorite human friends don't fit into a specific mold, so my fabric friends don't either.

With fabrics piled all around, I selected 25 that would form the center design. In rows of five by five, I put samples on my design wall, arranging and rearranging them for maximum contrast and interest. When I was sure of the arrangement, each fabric was assigned a number. Then it was easy to graph the design.

The blocks were paper pieced. The color number of each piece was written on the paper so I wouldn't get mixed up as the blocks were sewn. I began near the center of the quilt, and as each block was sewn, it went on my design wall to ensure that the twisting of the design matched my original idea.

When all blocks were finished, they were sewn together. Borders were added and I began quilting. That's when it hit me. The centers of each design were very large and ugly. What to do? I find that situations like this always bring out my best creativity.

Having always been fascinated by Celtic design, I had been reading and studying about this interesting, ancient art. Could it be possible for this contemporary color scheme to be combined with this old art form? Of course it could! The decor of my house is a mixture of antiques and contemporary art, so why not my quilt. I've always loved blending things that at first might not seem compatible. I was off to my quilt guild library to research the possibilities. Finding the perfect design wasn't quite as easy as it appeared. I used an old design, but modified it to fit the space.

I tried the Celtic design with traditional bias tape, but it lacked the impact the quilt deserved. With some experimenting, I found that a chenille strip was the answer. After many configurations, my solution was to use three 1¼" bias strips of the base color, topped with two ¾" bias strips of the top color. Stacking these together, I sewed the middle with a short stitch length. Being careful not to cut into the stitching, I clipped to the center line on both sides of the strip.

Next, the knot was enlarged to the correct size. Pinning the paper pattern to the ironing board, I wove the knots on the pattern, applied spray starch, and pressed them so they would keep their shape. When cool and stiff, I sewed the knots to the quilt as part of the quilting design. The border area is a modified design I created. After everything was quilted, the quilt was washed to remove the starch and to fluff the Celtic areas. The final step was a thorough vacuuming to get rid of all the lint.

Lucy's Celtic design, modified to fit the quilt

Judy Sogn

Seattle, Washington

Meet the Quilter

Constantly inspired and challenged by other quilts, I enjoy designing original works, but also enjoy recreating a pattern for an admired quilt. The joy is in the doing for me. I love trying my hand at all kinds of techniques and may only try something once, but finding out I can do it is rewarding. There are many things I can't do, and that makes me appreciate the work of others all the more.

After years of clothing construction, knitting, and needlepoint, I started quilting in 1982. Making things with my hands has always been a joy. Because of the large variety of techniques and so many different things to be made, I have remained a quilter all these years.

Quilting is a wonderful medium because I can make something original even though I'm not good at drawing or painting. While some friends dread retirement with nothing to do, I know there will always be some project on my to-do list. If I were to somehow reach the bottom of that list, there will be something new to inspire me just around the corner.

Primarily making wall quilts, I enjoy changing the quilts on my walls as the seasons change. I've nearly run out of walls for all my Christmas quilts, so they will have to be stacked here and there because I never tire of making them.

With computer software, I tried several methods of combining both designs in one block and settled on superimposing one block over the other.

Black & White & Red Allover

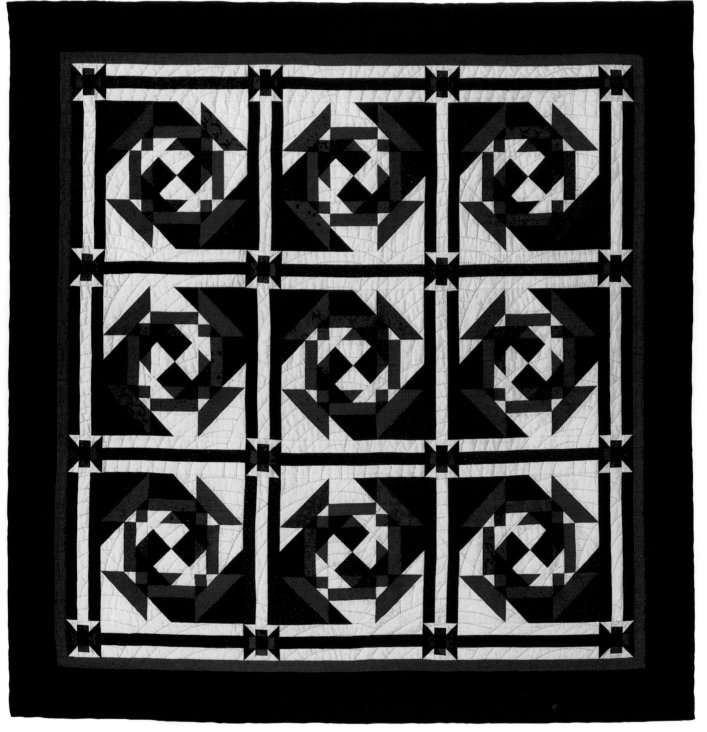

57" x 57"

INSPIRATION AND DESIGN

Working on a design for this year's contest, I wasn't sure which Monkey Wrench pattern was the intended focus of the competition. I decided to use the two designs that I associate with this block, which are Snail's Trail and Churn Dash.

With computer software, I tried several methods of combining both designs in one block and settled on superimposing one block over the other. This is a technique I've never tried and it makes the block easier to piece than with alternative designs. I colored every other patch red and the remaining patches either black or white, depending on their position in the Snail's Trail. The two blocks appear to be woven together.

The first time I colored the design on the computer, black and white were used for the Snail's Trail portion of the block because it was easy, quick, and the contrast showed the design well. With the addition of the red Monkey Wrench, I was happy with the design and never got around to trying other color combinations. I had my title when I remembered the old grade-school riddle, *What is black and white and red all over? A newspaper.*

The blocks were foundation paper pieced. I pieced the sashing and corner squares to form Monkey Wrenches between and around the blocks. For the back of the quilt, I pieced a large Monkey Wrench block with curved seams and found a wonderful black-and-white newspaper print for the background. For the label, two clip-art images were combined to form a monkey holding a monkey wrench. Finally, I hand quilted a fan design with red perle cotton thread over the entire quilt.

PAPER PIECING THE BLOCKS

Three different units are required for paper piecing the blocks. The center unit has two individual triangles that are attached after the rest of the center unit is sewn. The corner square block is paper pieced with two different units.

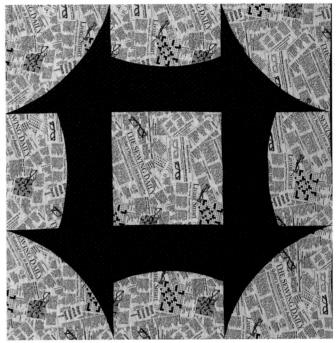

Photo of quilt back

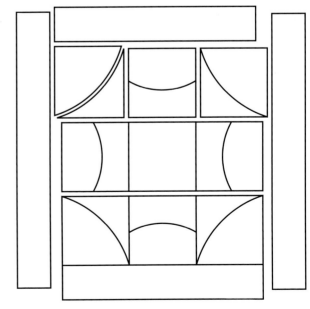

Assembly of quilt back

For the sashing, 42" x 1½" strips were cut and sewn into strip-sets. The color combinations of half the strip-sets are black-white-black and the other half are white-black-white. The strips-sets were then rotary cut to 12½" and placed so they form Monkey Wrench variations in the cornerstones.

To make a 12" block, enlarge the units 130%.

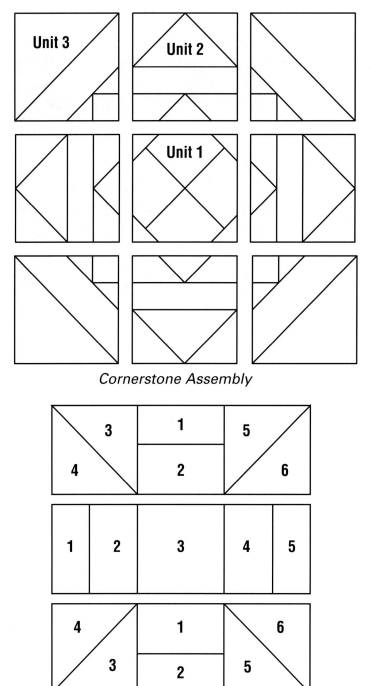

Cornerstone Assembly

Corner Square Assembly

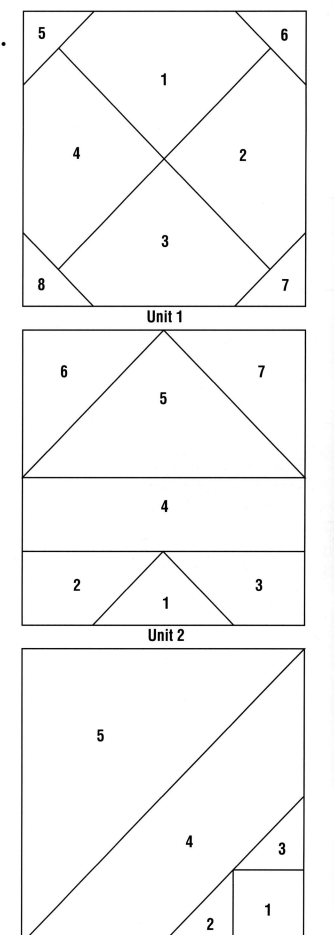

Unit 1

Unit 2

Unit 3

Kristina Chase Strom

Glendale, Ohio

To me, quiltmaking is at once personal and universal ... In my own humble way, I am participating in the conscious creation and continuation of history.

MEET THE QUILTER

Though not a part of my family tradition, quiltmaking has been one of my dreams almost as long as I can remember. For many years, I felt thwarted each time a step was made toward achieving this goal.

In the early 1970s, I built and lived in a log cabin near the Aiyansh Nishka Reserve in northern British Columbia. The closest town was 50 miles south on a treacherous logging road. Monthly treks to town involved careful planning and a certain risk, but were unavoidable for essential supplies. Stopping into a sparsely stocked sewing store was always first on my list. On one visit, tucked behind dust-covered notions, I found a pamphlet yellow with age titled *Patchwork Piecing*. My spirits soared! At last I had found instructions for making a quilt. After days of basting fabric squares into inexpertly crafted blocks, I gave up in despair. Making a quilt would surely take a lifetime, so I decided to focus on spinning and weaving.

In the mid-1970s, I moved back to the United States and enrolled at a college that was among the first liberal arts institutions offering a fiber art major. As an older student, I was welcomed by staff as a peer advisor and invited to informal planning sessions where the scope of this new program was discussed. Everything except quilting was offered. When I tentatively mentioned this omission, the group looked at me as though they perhaps had made a

Kismet

54½" x 63"

mistake in including me. Whispers circulated the table about a nationally known Ohio weaver who had recently "gone over" to quilting, stunning the fiber art world. She had clearly lost her mind! Privately, I was thrilled to learn that I wasn't alone in my dream and nascent passion.

Thirty years later, I still smile when recalling that gathering, unaware what a profound impact that scandalous news would have on my life. The quilting renaissance exploded a few short years after that time. I am heartened that the former schism between quilters and other fiber artists no longer exists, replaced by an exciting collaborative spirit and exchange that enhances and expands all of our work.

Looking back, I realize that quilting had become a centering principle without my knowing. As a single mom with four young daughters, most of what I did was invisible. All that was visible at the end of the day was what I hadn't done. Creating and completing a project, no matter how small, resulted in something tangible and lasting. When the girls were teenagers, quilting was how I retained a shred of sanity. Working on a quilt, whether by hand or machine, quiets my mind and soothes my soul. To me, quiltmaking is at once personal and universal. I feel connected with something greater than myself. In my own humble way, I am participating in the conscious creation and continuation of history.

After 26 years of active mothering, I have the luxury of time to pursue my passion daily. Like any endeavor, I go through periods of frustration and self-doubt, even to the point of wondering why I'm doing this. Unlike other endeavors, I awaken each morning ready to get back to work, which constantly amazes me. One thing I know to be true about the future is that I will always be quilting.

INSPIRATION AND DESIGN

A book I discovered before the quilting renaissance was Ruby McKim's *101 Patchwork Patterns* (Dover, 1962). I earmarked the Snail's Trail block long ago, but had yet to make it. I have an abiding fondness for the Churn Dash-style variation on the Monkey Wrench, because this is the pattern used in my first full-sized quilt. Upon learning the theme for the museum contest, I was immediately inspired.

My mind flooded with possibilities. I was driven to research the history of this block, in the course of which just about every phrase or sentiment about monkeys and wrenches assaulted my brain. Images floated in my head from E.M. Forrester's *A Passage to India,* in which hundreds of monkeys tumble out of an ancient temple. These images were juxtaposed by pioneers repairing wagon wheels. Within a few months, my project folder was over an inch thick with enough ideas for a lifetime of work, or at least a book.

In this frenzied space of overwhelm, I designed a medallion quilt incorporating both designs. I was pleased with the results as the quilt grew. Then in midsummer, I hit a wall. Not only was there a critical flaw in my design, but beyond the unique center medallion and first border, the quilt wasn't singing. My intended masterpiece looked abjectly ordinary. I spent the next three weeks frantically redrafting, redesigning, and resewing. Describing my emotional state as "freaked-out" would be an understatement. Defeated, I packed up the unfinished quilt, which I had never done before. Maybe I wasn't destined to enter the museum contest this year.

Several days later, I left for a long-awaited retreat in the country. For the first time ever, the only art-related supplies packed were some colored pencils and a pad of graph paper. Following several days of immersing myself in the glories of nature, I woke one morning filled with that joyous feeling of renewal. After breakfast, I poured a second cup of coffee and began to sketch, elongating the square Monkey Wrench pattern to 6" x 8". While arranging a stack of these rectangles, I cut several into segments on a whim and dubbed them "fragments of fate." While slicing away, I was also venting fury at this cherished block that had beguiled and betrayed me. Suddenly, the disappointment and frustration of the past few weeks faded away. By sunset, a design for the quilt emerged complete with a name that magically entered my mind during the course of the day: KISMET.

OVERCOMING OBSTACLES CREATIVELY

Before cutting and sewing, there were several obstacles to overcome. First, I had to isolate the individual fragments and determine how many were required, as well as organize the color configurations of each unit. Second, I needed to determine the most efficient construction for the separate components. Third, I had to develop a plan for joining the finished blocks.

I drew lines on the original sketch, but that didn't work, so I visited my local printer to have it reduced and copied several times. One copy was cut into fragments, then pasted onto poster board, leaving a white space between sections, creating a guide that would be my constant and invaluable reference during the entire process of construction (fig. 1).

Getting down to the nitty-gritty strategy of making each block, I drafted a line drawing on the computer for accuracy's sake to determine the exact size. I discovered that the angle of the center diamond Four-Patch was neither the standard 45 nor 60 degrees, but a funky 75. I used a compass, straight edge, and permanent fine-tip marker to draw a new angular line on my transparent ruler. This allowed me to strip piece two-color strata to

construct these units. Templates were made for the surrounding triangles.

I rolled up my sleeves and began to sew, making each fragment one at a time. While piecing the blocks by machine, I checked for accuracy often. The clock ticked away and the days on the calendar flew by with only the central motif of the quilt finished. By September, I knew a more streamlined approach was called for to meet the deadline.

My solution was to cut apart yet another copy of the original sketch and paste together a guide so primitive to the point of embarrassment (fig. 2, page 90). Regardless, using this new plan facilitated the construction of the central diamond Four-Patches and the cutting and stacking of the triangles. After assembly-line sewing all similar units, the blocks were complete and on the design wall.

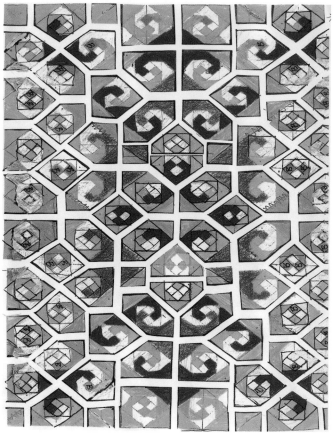

Fig. 1. Original sketch cut into fragments

From the moment my master working guide was pasted up, I noticed that a secondary parquetry-like design was created by the white spaces. While working on the top, I kept focusing on this unexpected element. My original plan was to piece the blocks in a traditional manner, but in doing so, this sculptural dimension would be lost. Though I thought my "shaggy chic" adventure was over, that method proved to be the solution.

Fortunately, the outside edges of the blocks had not been squared. I made eight plastic templates to cut out ⅜" seam allowances and guarantee uniformity (fig. 3). The next step was to cut backing and batting for the individual units. After layering, I machine quilted in the ditch around the patches and free-motion quilted a modified starburst in the outer triangles.

Assembling the 84 "quiltlets" was an exercise in Y and inset seams. Any fear I had about these some-times-tricky techniques was eradicated forever. After joining each unit, I fringed the exposed seams by cutting at scant ⅛" intervals.

The borders were constructed and quilted separately before connecting them to the body of the quilt. For binding, I used slightly larger-than-usual strips attached in the French manner. Washing the quilt several times enhanced the frayed edges. At last, KISMET was complete and I vowed never to question destiny again.

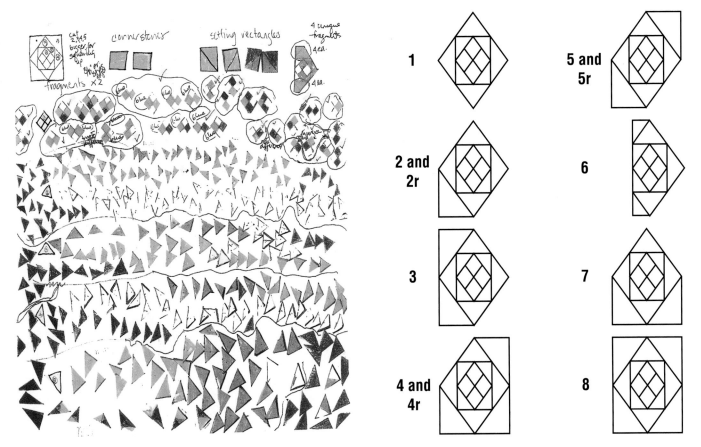

Fig. 2. Primitive guide to original cut-apart sketch

Fig. 3. Eight templates for the 84 "quiltlets"

Monkey Wrench Patterns

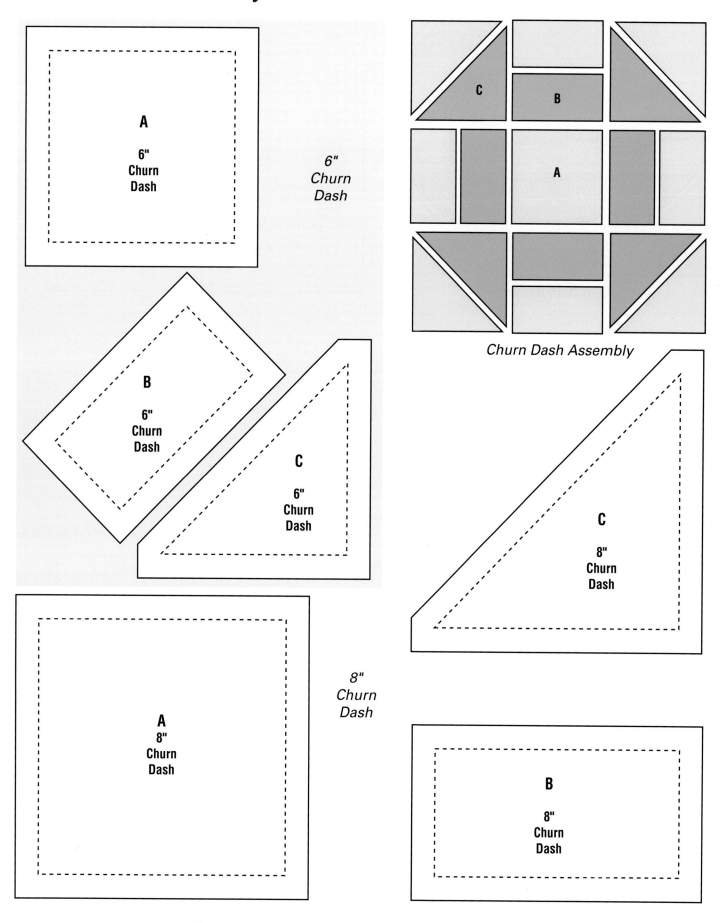

A
6"
Churn
Dash

6"
Churn
Dash

C
B

A

Churn Dash Assembly

B
6"
Churn
Dash

C
6"
Churn
Dash

C
8"
Churn
Dash

A
8"
Churn
Dash

8"
Churn
Dash

B
8"
Churn
Dash

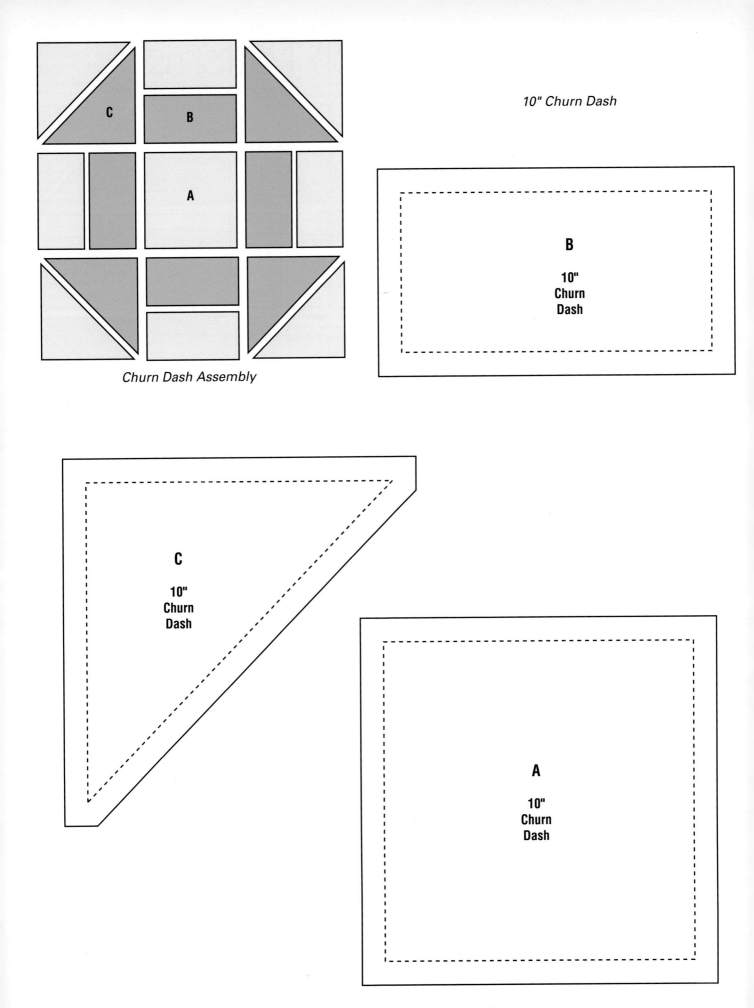

10" Churn Dash

C

10"
Churn
Dash

B

10"
Churn
Dash

A

10"
Churn
Dash

Churn Dash Assembly

MONKEY WRENCH: New Quilts from an Old Favorite

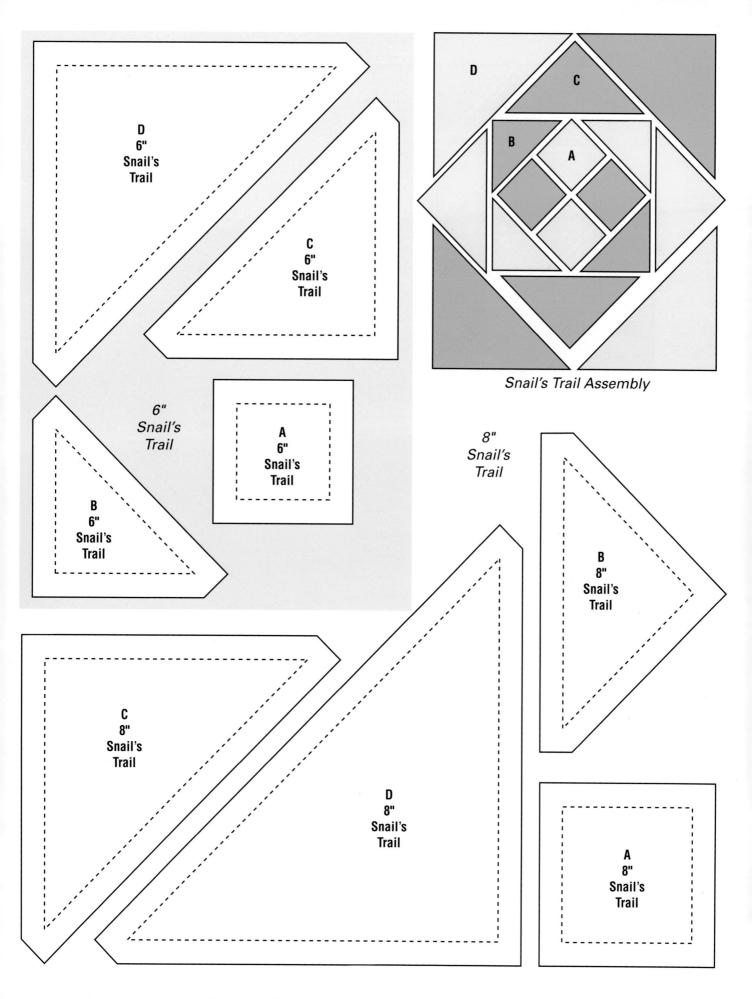

D
6"
Snail's
Trail

C
6"
Snail's
Trail

*6"
Snail's
Trail*

A
6"
Snail's
Trail

B
6"
Snail's
Trail

C
6"
Snail's
Trail

B
6"
Snail's
Trail

A
6"
Snail's
Trail

D

C

B

A

Snail's Trail Assembly

*8"
Snail's
Trail*

B
8"
Snail's
Trail

C
8"
Snail's
Trail

D
8"
Snail's
Trail

A
8"
Snail's
Trail

MONKEY WRENCH: New Quilts from an Old Favorite

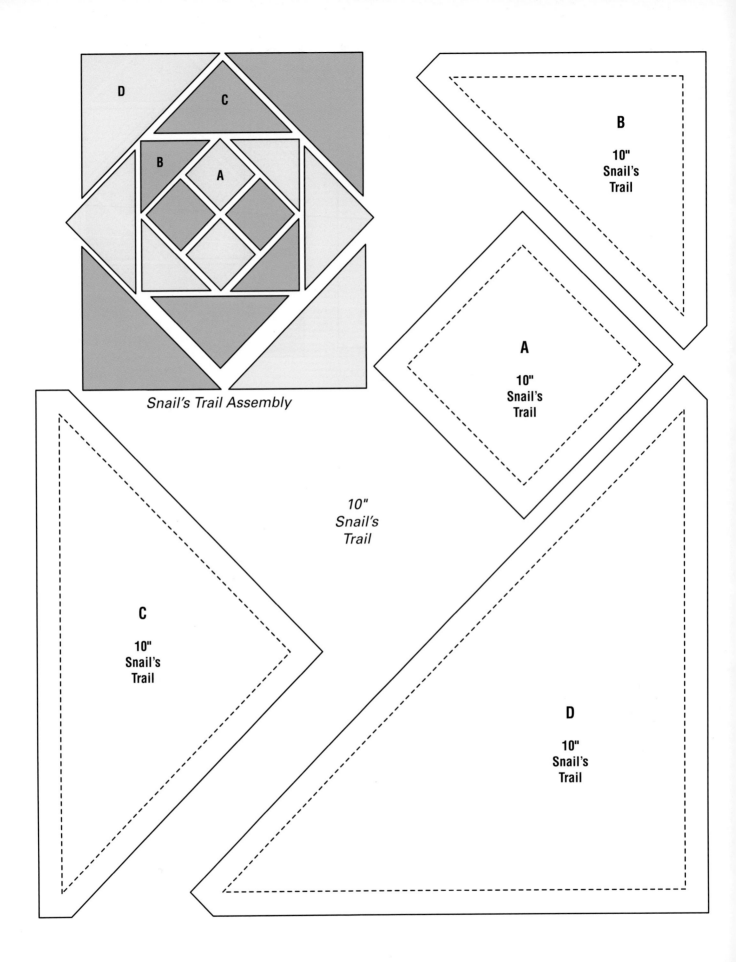

Snail's Trail Assembly

B

10"
Snail's
Trail

A

10"
Snail's
Trail

10"
Snail's
Trail

C

10"
Snail's
Trail

D

10"
Snail's
Trail

The Museum

The Museum of the American Quilter's Society (MAQS) is an exciting place where the public can learn more about quilts, quilt-making, and quiltmakers. Founded in 1991 by Bill and Meredith Schroeder as a not-for-profit organization, MAQS is located in an expansive 27,000 square-foot facility, making it the largest quilt museum in the world. Its facility includes three exhibit galleries, four classrooms, and a gift and book shop.

Through collecting quilts and other programs, MAQS focuses on celebrating and developing today's quiltmaking. It provides a comprehensive program of exhibits, activities, events, and services to educate about the ever-developing art and tradition of quiltmaking. Whether presenting new or antique quilts, MAQS promotes understanding of, and respect for, all quilts – new and antique, traditional and innovative, machine made and handmade, utility and art.

The MAQS exhibit galleries regularly feature a selection of the museum's own collection of quilts made from the 1980s on, as well as exhibits of new and antique quilts and related archival materials. Work-shops, conferences, and exhibit-related publications provide additional educational opportunities. The museum's shop carries a wide selection of fine crafts and hundreds of quilt and textile books.

Located in historic downtown Paducah, Kentucky, MAQS is open year-round 10 A.M. to 5 P.M. Monday through Saturday. From April 1 through October 31, it is also open on Sundays from 1 to 5 P.M. The entire facility is wheelchair accessible.

MAQS programs can also be enjoyed on the Web site: www.quiltmuseum.org or through MAQS traveling exhibits, like the New Quilts from an Old Favorite contest and exhibit. For more information, write MAQS, PO Box 1540, Paducah, KY 42002-1540; phone (270) 442-8856; or e-mail: info@quiltmuseum.org.

Other AQS Books

This is only a small selection of the books available from the American Quilter's Society. AQS books are known worldwide for timely topics, clear writing, beautiful color photos, and accurate illustrations and patterns. The following books are available from your local bookseller, quilt shop, or public library.